THE BLACK BOX

Malcolm MacPherson is an American author who has published works of non-fiction, as well as novels. He is also prolific as a magazine and newspaper journalist, having been published in, amongst others, *Newsweek*, *New York* magazine and the *International Herald Tribune*.

THE BLACK BOX

COCKPIT VOICE RECORDER
ACCOUNTS OF IN-FLIGHT ACCIDENTS

EDITED BY MALCOLM MacPHERSON

HarperCollins*Publishers*

HarperCollins*Publishers*
77–85 Fulham Palace Road,
Hammersmith, London W6 8JB
http://www.harpercollins.co.uk

Published by HarperCollins*Publishers* 1998
3 5 7 9 8 6 4

Published by arrangement with William Morrow and Company, Inc.

Copyright © Malcolm MacPherson 1998

The author asserts the moral right to
be identified as the author of this work

A catalogue record for this book is
available from the British Library

ISBN 0 00 653045 1

Set in Sabon by
Rowland Phototypesetting Ltd,
Bury St Edmunds, Suffolk

Printed and bound in Great Britain by
Scotprint Ltd, Musselburgh, Scotland.

CONTENTS

INTRODUCTION

Nearly everyone who has ever flown on a scheduled commercial flight has experienced the fear of flying. Whether in clear skies or cloudy, during a routine flight or in an emergency, we have shared a common feeling of dread, usually attended by clammy palms, whitened knuckles and wildly racing hearts.

What lies behind this, of course, is the threat of injury or an unimaginably grim death, which the primitive stem of our brains that oversees our basic instincts for survival tells us may be the consequence of such an unnatural act for us humans. *It* knows we have no wings and those are *clouds* under us.

No education or sophistication, no reassuring baritone over the public address system, no number of highballs and no degree of embarrassment can seem to quell this fear when it comes to haunt us in those minutes between take-off and landing. A gust of wind violently shakes the airframe in which we are held virtual prisoners and no mantra-like recitation of safety facts will quiet the terrified voice inside of each of us which is saying, 'I *really* don't want to be here.'

Still, the truism applies: besides propulsion on our own two legs, the safest means of transportation is aboard a commercial airliner. As confusing as it may seem to our sense of logic, a commercial flight is safer even than eating, which should be food for thought the next time you are being served an in-flight meal.

Thanks to the high level of professionalism of aircraft manufacturers, airlines (through their entire hierarchy), and especially of the airlines' flight crews, plus the vigilance of the Federal Aviation Administration (FAA), and the attention to detail of the National Transportation Safety Board (NTSB), aviation accidents have (and I apologize for this word) plummeted since the advent of big-jet travel in the early 1960s.

In America, about 100 people die *on average* each year in commercial airline accidents. In 1996, a year of higher than average aviation death tolls, 1,187 people were killed on commercial jet flights *worldwide* in Western-built jets (394 people died in America, reflecting mostly two accidents – TWA 800 off Long Island with 230 fatalities and ValuJet in Florida with 110 fatalities). That 394 compares with 19,000 Americans that year who were murdered, 41,907 who succumbed in automobile accidents, and 714 who died in boating mishaps. In 1993, one (1) person died in an aviation-related incident in America; and he was struck by a whirring propeller blade while standing on the ground.

In sum, for every million commercial airline hours flown, the fatal accident rate in the United States has fluctuated over the recent decades from a low of 0.013 to a high of 0.7; it was .439 in 1996, which was the fifth highest in the last 15 years. In Europe the average was 0.9, and in Australia, 0.3. In regions of South America and Africa, China and Russia, the rates rise. In Africa as a whole, there is an average of 13 fatal accidents per million hours; in South America, 5.7, according to the Flight Safety Foundation in Alexandria, Virginia.

Accidents are so rare in America and Europe that virtually anything that the authorities and the airlines do to make flying safer will not reduce the accident rate by any appreciable statistical means. Yet as more and more people in parts of the world outside America and Europe begin to fly, according to a 1996 report in the *New York Times*, 'the industry will have to lower its accident rate just to keep the number of crashes roughly constant each year'. The *New York Times* report (9 December 1996) then reached an ominous conclusion. 'If the current accident rate remains steady and air travel continues to grow rapidly, a passenger jet may crash as often as once a week by the year 2010'.

Yet it is important to keep this perspective in mind: Flying in most 'dangerous' parts of the world is still far, far safer than driving a car in the United States.

The commercial aviation industry is constantly striving to make air travel safer. An enormous amount of work is constantly underway to find ways to improve safety. Wind shear *was* a big problem, but after several fatal wind shear-related accidents (like Delta No. 191 at Dallas–Fort Worth in August 1985), the industry sought to understand the phenomenon, how it forms, and what pilots should do about it. As a result, techniques to fly out of wind shear were developed. Now, with the help of research and new technologies, wind shear incidents have decreased substantially. Add to that the introduction of passive safety measures like ground proximity warning systems shouting at pilots to pull up, floor lighting in cabins to direct passengers during emergency exits, smoke retardants in manufactured materials, and aids like smoke detectors and fire extinguishers in bathrooms and in air-freight holds, and flying just keeps getting safer, in spite of burgeoning numbers of world flight departures and passengers.

Why then does the craven voice in our heads keep telling us when we are flying, 'I *really* don't want to be here?'

For one thing, statistics are other people. For another, the media blow their coverage of air fatalities out of all proportion to their coverage of other forms of transportation deaths, and they frighten us. (When was the last time that the report of an automobile accident, except for that of Diana, Princess of Wales appeared on the front page of the *New York Times*?) The media rationale is clear: When there is a commercial airplane accident, it often means a mass destruction of human life. This also may provide the media with mysteries that resist a simple solution, like TWA 800, the Boeing 747 that exploded after take-off from JFK International Airport in 1996; the destruction of 800's hull involved an unexplained, instantaneous horror that remains an enigma. With the ValuJet crash in the Everglades on 11 May 1996, the hull was swallowed up in a swamp teeming with alligators, and until oxygen generators were discovered as the culprit, the crash offered what looked like a very dark mystery. And the crash in Pittsburgh of USAir 427 on 8 September 1994, still stubbornly defies a simple explanation for the loss of those 132 lives.

In the case of those that are easily explained, there is no denying that airline disasters hold a fascination for the media and the public alike that we can't really explain.

The airlines do all they can to reassure us with more than statistics and soothing words. They try to get passengers involved; they want us to *think* safety. There are obvious practical reasons behind seat belts, No Smoking signs, floor exit light strips, and straight seat backs during the critical flight periods of take-off and landing; cabin crews do not repeat procedures with oxygen masks, flotation devices, and emergency exits without the certain awareness that these measures can prevent accidents and save lives. These measures also reassure us by telling us indirectly that the airline is concerned about our safety. Indeed, we may think we even hold a modicum of control over our destinies with our seatbelts snugly around our laps. So it is also with the cockpit crews who reassure us in soothing, authoritative tones over the public address system, even when – especially when – they may be frenzied in an emergency.

Contributing to the mystery of our fears, while we may feel nothing out of the ordinary in the passenger cabin, a drama we may never suspect may be unfolding in the cockpit. When things go wrong behind that closed door, often one crippled or failed mechanical system collapses on another. Suddenly, horns blare, recorded voices shout 'Terrain! Terrain! Pull Up! Pull Up!' Lights flash before the flight crew's eyes. Confusion often results; automatic responses are triggered in men and women who are more highly trained, retrained and scrutinized regularly for their performances than any other professionals in our society including heart surgeons. In a truly amazing number of incidents that we may never read about, these crews bring their airplanes back to land safely, without the passengers even being aware that their lives were at risk.

In a tiny percentage of flights, airplanes crash; passengers die. The one true record of what went wrong is contained in recorders called 'black boxes', which federal authorities have required since 1957 as standard equipment aboard all commercial aircraft over a certain weight. Actually the boxes are painted a bright international orange with two white diagonal stripes for easy recognition and the words stencilled in black, 'flight recorder do not open'. And on the other side of the outer box the words are in French 'en registreur de vol ne pas ouvrir'.

The black box holds two components: the Flight Data Recorder (FDR) keeps a record of the airframe's performance – its compass headings, airspeeds, altitude levels, vertical acceleration, and microphone keying, among other things; the second component, required by federal law in commercial aircraft since 1966, is the Cockpit Voice Recorder (CVR), which weighs 21.5 pounds and records the sounds in the cockpit.

Within the orange outer CVR black box, a separate box of welded quarter-inch stainless steel protects (from up to 3,300 gs of force) a self-erasing, 30-minute magnetic tape loop, which is being replaced in all new commercial aircraft by a two-hour self-erasing solid-state recorder. Black boxes are fitted in the tails of airframes; cables down the length of the fuselage connect them to one-inch circular microphones in the overhead area of the cockpit and the 'boom mikes' (like the microphone that the pop singer Madonna wears in her live performances) which FAA law requires Pilots and Co-pilots to wear while flying under 18,000 feet of altitude. Both black boxes (CVR, FDR) contain underwater locator beacons, which emit ultrasonic pings every second for sixty days after a crash, to help rescuers find them. The boxes are incredibly resilient. The force of impact has never destroyed one, even the recorder that sustained a crushing 9,000 gs of impact on board the hijacked PSA flight that crashed in 1987 near San Luis Obisbo; fires rendered a few of the recorders useless before new federal fire regulations upgraded them a few years ago. And only one set of boxes is still lost on the ocean floor – that of an Alitalia jet that is thought to have been shot down by Moammar Gadhafi's air force off Libya in the Mediterranean Sea more than a decade ago.

I first started reading the transcripts of CVR tapes when I was living in Nairobi and working as a correspondent there for *Newsweek*. I never thought of myself as a ghoul for this unusual fascination. Far from it. I was able to picture the drama of what these transcripts contained, and these were unlike any I had ever read, seen on the screen, or watched in a theater. They were *real*, relived on the printed page.

Originally, I picked up the transcripts out of a concern about my own safety in the air. In those days I was taking off and landing in places and on airplanes that would naturally raise the fears in any sane person (I once took off from Nouakchott, Mauritania, with live chickens in the cabin, and as we zoomed down the runway I spied a silver puddle on the taxiway out in the Saharan sun that I recognized as my Zero Haliburton suitcase). In those days I believed that the more I learned about the behavior of crews in accident environments, the less I would fear flying.

Since then, I have tried to read the findings of the NTSB for most major commercial airplane accidents. Nothing I can think of has given me a better feel for what things are like up there when things go wrong. Unfortunately, while the transcripts continue to hold my interest for their drama, they have not lessened my fear of flying. (When I read recently how the cockpit crew in a China Northern Boeing MD-82 over western China in November 1993, lost track of their altitude in the fog on a landing approach – and when the recorded ground-proximity warning system warned them in English to 'Pull up . . . Pull up', the Pilot was overheard later on the CVR, after they had crashed, asking his Co-pilot in Chinese, 'What means "Pull up"?' – I wondered whether my fears were not well founded, even if I never plan to fly anywhere near China ever.)

No, the CVR transcripts have certainly not allayed my fears, nor probably will they yours. But they often can go a long way to explain in the most graphic and dramatic terms the professionalism – if not the outright heroism – of many commercial pilots and crews and the extraordinary measures they take to ensure our safety.

In the transcripts you are about to read, I have made no effort to 'characterize' the crew members whose voices are taken directly off the CVR tapes. I do not want these transcripts to seem like an airport novel of Arthur Hailey, as good as those may be. Whether the captain of the airplane is kind to animals, is married with children, et cetera, does not seem relevant to me in an accident environment; the same with the passengers whose lives are unknown to me. But I have tried to give the readers a context (of weather outside the airframe, of time, of the numbers in the cabin, the sights and the sounds). I edited some of the dialogue for clarity and understanding and I have put some of the pilots' jargon in brackets in laymen's terms; a glossary serves as a further aid to understanding.

The readers of *The Black Box* might be advised to imagine themselves, rather than riding in these airplanes, tuned to an emergency frequency on a radio. You are overhearing – albeit *reading* – the conversations between the crew members in the cockpit of an airplane in an emergency and, from time to time, conversations between the cockpit and the ground controllers who are giving assistance to the crippled flight. Even if you cannot visualize everything, I hope you will agree with my long-standing conviction that these transcripts are as dramatic reading as you are likely to find, because they are the minute-to-minute unvarnished accounts of what actually happened.

Malcolm MacPherson
email: m.macpherson@erols.com

I have chosen to lead the collection with this CVR tape because it shows how a cockpit crew, by their skill and resourcefulness, saved the passengers from what was certain disaster.

Aboard American Airlines Flight 1572 that blustery fall evening there were 73 passengers, including one child, with a flight crew of three Flight Attendants, a Pilot and Co-pilot who had left Chicago's O'Hare International Airport at 11.05 p.m. after a two hour delay. The flight to Hartford, Connecticut's Bradley International Airport (BDL) was for the most part uneventful, although the captain changed from a flight altitude of 33,000 feet to 35,000 feet to avoid turbulence. For the most part, the passengers rode comfortably.

Near the flight's conclusion, about 300 miles from the airport, Flight 1572 was cleared direct to Bradley. Outside the aircraft, a low pressure area that extended south from Quebec over New York City caused strong southerly and westerly winds and rain. At times at the airport toward which Flight 1572 was heading, the winds gusted to 49 mph. As the flight approached BDL, the crew received two messages: one notifying them of a changed altimeter setting, and another which warned of turbulence and wind shear on final approach.

At 12.32, the flight descended to 19,000 feet. Severe turbulence was reported below 10,000 feet. At 32:23 minutes past midnight, the Captain advised the flight crew to secure the cabin because of the anticipated turbulence. The crew was briefed by ground controllers to approach Runway 15. At 12.45, the crew was further advised by Bradley's approach control to descend to 4,000 feet. Four minutes later, the flight crew was told that the Tower was closing temporarily to repair a window that was loosened by the high winds.

On its landing approach the aircraft went below the minimum descent altitude of 1,008 feet. The Pilot glanced out of the window. When he looked back at his instruments, the airplane was flying at only 350 feet – only five seconds away from hitting a cluster of tall conifer trees near the end of Runway 15. An outdated altimeter setting had allowed the autopilot to descend the aircraft about 309 feet below the indicated minimum descent altitude. The leading and the trailing edges of the wings sheared off the tops of the trees. Power from one engine failed almost instantly; power from the other engine failed shortly thereafter.

We pick up the CVR tape as the flight is just starting its descent into Bradley.

FLIGHT ATTENDANT TO CAPTAIN ON INTERCOM: Were you looking for me?
CAPTAIN: We just got the message. It's . . . going to be real bumpy on the way down to landing.
FLIGHT ATTENDANT: Okay.
CAPTAIN: So put everything away or whatever as soon as we start down. Uh, matter of fact, we're starting our descent now. So you can lock it all up and prepare for landing.
FLIGHT ATTENDANT: Okay, thank you.
CAPTAIN TO CO-PILOT: Let's go down.
CO-PILOT: Out of three five oh [35,000 feet] for flight level one nine oh [19,000], American fifteen seventy-two.

CAPTAIN TO CO-PILOT: You might want to cool it down too. It's gonna get bumpy [and the passengers will] be throwing up.

Bradley Tower advises American 1572 that there is now severe turbulence below 10,000 feet.

BRADLEY: Bradley Airport Information Victor, zero three five one . . . temperature six two, dew point five seven, wind one six zero at two-eight, gust three niner, altimeter two niner five zero. Approach in use, ILS [Instrument Landing System] Runway Twenty-four or VOR Runway Fifteen.

A minute later, the Co-pilot calls Bradley for another report on the weather at the airport. The information about wind shear and severe turbulence is reported.

CAPTAIN TO PASSENGERS ON PUBLIC ADDRESS SYSTEM: We've started our descent. Now we're about a hundred miles away from Bradley Field right now. Be touching down in about twenty-five minutes or so . . . And the latest temperature's sixty-two degrees and just calling it, uh, light rain. However, the winds, [are] pretty, uh, pretty high. They're saying the winds are up to thirty miles an hour or so. So it might get a little choppy right now. They're reporting some moderate turbulence on the descent. Might just get a little choppy on the way down.

CAPTAIN TO CO-PILOT: Just watch me the whole way, all right?

CO-PILOT: Yeah, man. You got it.

CAPTAIN: Any comments, scream out.

CO-PILOT: You're going to get a lot of turbulence. You know how to land it. I'll tell you, when I was an engineer, new with the airlines, I watched a guy. He's, uh – nobody likes him. He's a [Boeing] seven-two [seven], Captain. I forgot his damn name. All the [former] Navy guys, man, they hate his guts. He's still on the seven-two [seven]. He thinks he's an IP [Instructor Pilot] at the RAG [Training Squadron].

CAPTAIN: Uh.

CO-PILOT: I watched him land in thirty knots of direct cross [wind] up at Bradley when I was a wrench [flight engineer], and it scared the hell out of me. Actually it scared me bad. Some of the flying we do here [at Bradley] is much harder than . . .

CAPTAIN: Yeah, yeah, I agree, I agree.

CO-PILOT: Just fight'n it all the way down.

CAPTAIN: Oh, what gate are we goin' into?

CO-PILOT: Gate eight.

CAPTAIN: Gettin' a lotta rain out there.

CO-PILOT: Altimeters?

CAPTAIN: I'll tell you, flying at night. I don't like it worth a damn. [Altimeters at] Twenty-nine fifty?

CO-PILOT: Yeah, they called twenty-nine forty-seven when we started down.

CAPTAIN: Okay.

CO-PILOT: Pumps are up. You want these lights?

CAPTAIN: I think we can leave them [lights] off for now.

CAPTAIN GETS ON PUBLIC ADDRESS SYSTEM: Flight Attendants prepare for landing, please.

COCKPIT: [Sound of yawn]

CAPTAIN TO CO-PILOT: What's the overcast?

CO-PILOT: Twenty-seven hundred [2,700 feet].

BRADLEY APPROACH CONTROL: American fifteen seventy-two, fly heading of, uh, one zero zero.

CO-PILOT: One zero zero, American fifteen seventy-two.

CAPTAIN: One zero zero, one oh nine, one forty-eight. I'll use medium brakes.

CO-PILOT: Can't see [the airport] yet.

CAPTAIN: Lotta rain.

CO-PILOT: I can see that.

BRADLEY APPROACH CONTROL: American fifteen seventy-two, descend and maintain four thousand [4,000 feet].

CO-PILOT: Eleven for four thousand, American fifteen seventy-two.

BRADLEY: American fifteen seventy-two, the winds are one-seven-zero at two-nine, gust three-nine.

CO-PILOT: Copy.

COCKPIT: [Sound of laughter]

CAPTAIN: How about slats [forward edge flaps on wings]. Extend [them], please.

COCKPIT: [Sound of rattling similar to aircraft going through turbulence]

CO-PILOT: Approaching four thousand [feet of altitude].

CAPTAIN: Okay. Slowing down.

BRADLEY: American fifteen seventy-two, you're five miles from [final approach] at or above three thousand five hundred feet, cleared for VOR. Runway Fifteen approach.

CO-PILOT: Okay, we're cleared for the approach, and we'll cross the [final] at or above, uh, thirty-five hundred. American fifteen seventy-two.

CAPTAIN: Set. Comin' down.

BRADLEY: American fifteen seventy-two, be advised the Tower is closed at this time. It's a temporary closure, due to a problem with one of the windows, so I'll need a down time on you, but you can stay on this frequency for that.

CO-PILOT: Roger. What happened on the window?

BRADLEY: It's just loose. They've got carpenters up there now boarding it up . . . But once that's done the Tower should be open.

CO-PILOT: Copy.

CAPTAIN: Flaps eleven, please.

CO-PILOT: You got it.

COCKPIT: [Sound similar to aircraft going through turbulence]

CO-PILOT: Okay, thirty-five hundred feet. Looking good . . . I think it's gonna be smoother once we get out of the weather.

CAPTAIN: Yeah.

CO-PILOT: Okay, you're at thirty-five hundred.

CAPTAIN: Okay, we're cleared down to where?

CO-PILOT: You're cleared down to two thousand . . .

CAPTAIN: Okay, two thousand set and armed.

CO-PILOT: Five miles, so it's good. Two thousand is set and armed.

CAPTAIN: Flaps fifteen [lower flaps].

CO-PILOT: Down to flaps fifteen.

COCKPIT: [Sound similar to flap/slat handle being moved and sound of rattling similar to aircraft going through turbulence]

CAPTAIN: Okay, comin' down.

CO-PILOT: Ten miles.

CAPTAIN: Comin' back to idle.

CO-PILOT: Roger.

BRADLEY: American fifteen seventy-two, you show yourself on the final? Looks like you're uh, a bit to the left of it.

CO-PILOT: Copy.

CAPTAIN: Yeah, looks like we're to the left of it.

BRADLEY: American fifteen seventy-two, roger, and the wind's now one seven zero at two four, gust three five [35 mph].

CO-PILOT: Roger.

CAPTAIN: How about [landing] gear down, please.

COCKPIT: [Sound similar to landing gear handle being operated, followed by sound similar to nose gear door opening]

CO-PILOT: Thousand and five.

BRADLEY: American fifteen seventy-two, there is someone [back] in the Tower. It's not really officially open, but you can change to Tower frequency, one two zero point three.

CO-PILOT: Okay, you're not gonna need that down time [in the Tower]?

BRADLEY: Negative.

CO-PILOT: See ya.

BRADLEY: Good day.

CAPTAIN: Okay, it's two thousand feet until five miles [from runway].

CO-PILOT: That's it.

CAPTAIN: Comin' back. Flaps twenty-eight.

COCKPIT: [Sound similar to flaps handle being moved]

CO-PILOT: Okay, going down to nine oh eight [908 feet], huh?

CAPTAIN: Yeah.

CO-PILOT: Set and armed. VOR right on track.

CAPTAIN: Okay.

CO-PILOT: Gear's down and green spoiler lever?

COCKPIT: [Sound of click similar to spoiler lever being armed]

CAPTAIN: Armed.

CO-PILOT: You got brakes . . . [Brakes] are going to be medium.

CO-PILOT TO BRADLEY: Hey, Tower, American fifteen seventy-two, we're on a six miles final for Runway Fifteen.

BRADLEY: American fifteen seventy-two, landing is at your discretion, sir. The wind at one seven zero at two five, peak gust to four zero . . . and uh, the runway does appear clear. You can land and taxi to the gate at your discretion.

CO-PILOT TO CAPTAIN: Showing you going through the course.

CO-PILOT TO BRADLEY: What are you showing right now for winds?

BRADLEY: One seven zero at two four.

CO-PILOT: Copy.

COCKPIT: [Sound of rattling similar to aircraft going through turbulence]

CAPTAIN: Flaps forty.

COCKPIT: [Sound of click similar to flap/slat handle being moved]

CO-PILOT: Annunciator lights checked, flaps and slats at forty forty and land. You're cleared to land, dude.

CAPTAIN: Okay, give me a thousand down.

CO-PILOT: One thousand down. You got it.

BRADLEY: Wind shear alert, uh, center field one seven zero at two five. The north-east boundary, one seven zero at two four, one niner zero at twelve at the south-east boundary.

CO-PILOT: Copy.

CO-PILOT TO CAPTAIN: There's a thousand feet. You got forty forty land, cleared to land.

CAPTAIN: Okay.

CO-PILOT: Nine hundred and eight feet is your, uh . . .

CAPTAIN: Right.

CO-PILOT: Your bug [limit].

COCKPIT: [Sound similar to turbulence]

CO-PILOT: You're going below your [limit].

COCKPIT RECORDED MECHANICAL VOICE: *Sink rate, sink rate.*

COCKPIT: [Sound of first impact]

At little more than 900 feet above the ground and 2.54 miles from the approach end of Runway 15, American 1572 clipped the top of the trees, then swerved sharply left then sharply right, then left again in line with the runway.

COCKPIT RECORDED MECHANICAL VOICE: *Sink rate* [sound of four beeps], *wind shear, wind shear, wind shear.*

CO-PILOT: Go, go around.

At this point, the Captain pushed the throttle full open to abort the landing. Landing gear was put up and flaps were brought back to 15° from 40.

CAPTAIN: We're going, going, going around, going around . . .

COCKPIT RECORDED MECHANICAL VOICE: *Landing gear* [sound of horn, sound of four beeps], *wind shear, wind shear, wind shear.*

CAPTAIN: Flaps fifteen, positive rate [they are climbing], gear up.

COCKPIT RECORDED MECHANICAL VOICE: *Landing gear.*

CO-PILOT: You want the gear up?

CAPTAIN: Yep.

COCKPIT RECORDED MECHANICAL VOICE: [Sound of horn] *Landing gear, landing gear.*

A couple of seconds after shearing off the tree tops, the airspeed started to decrease because of the damage to the two engines, and the airplane began a slow descent. The rain had stopped. The Co-pilot saw the runway ahead.

CAPTAIN: Left motor's failed.

CO-PILOT: There's the runway straight ahead.

CAPTAIN: Okay. Tell 'em [Bradley Tower] we're goin' down. Tell 'em Emergency.

CO-PILOT TO BRADLEY: Tower call for emergency equipment. We're going down on the runway.

CO-PILOT TO CAPTAIN: You want the [landing] gear back down?

CAPTAIN: Yes, throw it down!

COCKPIT RECORDED MECHANICAL VOICE: *Sink rate, sink rate, sink rate, sink rate.*

CAPTAIN: Oh, God.

CO-PILOT: You're gonna make it.

CAPTAIN: Okay.

COCKPIT RECORDED MECHANICAL VOICE: *Sink rate, sink rate.*

CO-PILOT: Flaps?

CAPTAIN: Put 'em down. What we got?

CO-PILOT: We're still flying.

CAPTAIN: Okay. God . . .

CO-PILOT: Keep coming.

COCKPIT RECORDED MECHANICAL VOICE: *Sink rate, too low, flaps, terrain, terrain, terrain, too low.*

CO-PILOT TO BRADLEY: Call for emergency, call for emergency equipment.

BRADLEY: They're coming, they're comin'.

COCKPIT RECORDED MECHANICAL VOICE: *Terrain, too low.*

CO-PILOT: You got it, dude. You're gonna make it.

CAPTAIN: Okay. Flaps forty. All the way down.

COCKPIT RECORDED MECHANICAL VOICE: *Don't sink.*

CAPTAIN: All the way, flaps forty.

CO-PILOT: They're all the way.

CAPTAIN: Okay, hold on, guy.

COCKPIT: [Sound of impact, this time with the ILS antenna sticking up near the end of the runway]

CAPTAIN: Hold it down, buddy, hold it down, hold it down, hold it down, hold it down . . .

Flight 1572 slammed down on the runway.

CO-PILOT: God bless you. You made it.

COCKPIT RECORDED MECHANICAL VOICE: *Landing gear.*

The airplane rolled to a stop on the runway.

COCKPIT: [Sound similar to engine rpm decreasing]

CAPTAIN: Shut down the motors.

CO-PILOT: Pull 'em both?

CAPTAIN: Yeah, pull both the fire handles.

END OF TAPE

The passengers and the crew members evacuated the airplane via the inflated door slides. There were no fatalities and only one minor injury to the passengers. Damage to the airplane was estimated at $9 million.

This is one of the more wrenching CVRs in this collection. It chronicles the fate of AeroPeru Flight 603 from Lima, Peru, to Santiago, Chile.

Earlier that day, the ground crew at Lima International Airport, while washing the fuselage of the AeroPeru Boeing 757, had taped over the aircraft's left-side static ports with masking tape. These ports, the small metal 'probes' that stick out of the fuselage of airplanes near the nose, read the ambient temperature, air pressure and measured wind speed. With tape covering the openings, the static ports could not function. And for the sophisticated Boeing 757 it was a little like being blind.

The ground crew had failed to remove the tape from the ports when they had finished washing the aircraft. And during their pre-flight visual check 'walk around' of the aircraft the cockpit crew of Flight 603 failed to take notice of the tape.

As a result, the flight took off that night without instruments to read air speed or altitude. While the crew had the ability to control the aircraft, the autopilot and auto-throttle computer controls lacked the data to operate with any accuracy.

From the start, the crew struggled to make sense of the perilous situation for twenty-eight minutes, as the aircraft veered over the Pacific, changing course and altitude several times. The 61 passengers and seven Flight Attendants were never told what was wrong.

We pick up the CVR as the Flight 603 is cleared for take-off.

CO-PILOT TO TOWER: Lima Tower, AeroPeru six zero three, Runway Fifteen, ready for take-off.

TOWER: AeroPeru six zero three, use noise attenuation, wind calm. You are authorized to take-off Runway Fifteen.

PILOT: One five, one five, transponder.

CO-PILOT: Flaps one five, take off briefing complete. Time check.

PILOT: Let's go.

COCKPIT: [Sound similar to engines accelerating]

PILOT: Power's set.
CO-PILOT: Power's set.
PILOT: Eighty knots.
CO-PILOT: Checked.
PILOT: Vee one.
PILOT: Rotate.
PILOT: Vee two.
PILOT: Positive [climb rate].
CO-PILOT: Gear up.
COCKPIT: [Sound similar to landing gear control moving]
PILOT: Right, vee two plus ten.
CO-PILOT: The altimeters are stuck!

This was the crew's first observation that their instruments were inoperative.

COCKPIT: [Sound similar to wind shear alarm]
CO-PILOT: Hey, altimeters have stuck!
PILOT: Yeah.
CO-PILOT: All of them?
PILOT: This is really new . . . Keep vee two plus ten . . . Vee two plus ten.
CO-PILOT: The speed . . .
PILOT: Eh?
CO-PILOT: The speed . . .
PILOT: Yeah right, vee two plus ten . . . What happened, [we're] not climbing?
CO-PILOT: I'm climbing, but the speed?

PILOT: Hold it, no . . . Keep the speed. Positive, eh, put ten degrees. We are descending.
CO-PILOT: Rudder ratio.

At this point the rudder ratio alarm sounded, indicating abnormal operation of speed sensors. This warns the Pilot to avoid large or abrupt rudder inputs. This is one of the signals that will hold the attention of the pilots throughout the emergency.

PILOT: How strange . . . Turn to the right . . . Well . . . Go up! Go up! Go up! Go up! Go up! Go up!
CO-PILOT: I'm . . .
PILOT: Go up! You are going down . . .
CO-PILOT: I am up, but the speed . . .
PILOT: Yeah, but it's [speedometer is] stuck . . . Mach trim, rudder ratio . . . Now you are . . . Go up! Go up! Go up! Go up! Go up heading one hundred . . . Eh . . . It's okay, this course.
CO-PILOT: Put the . . . Climb thrust . . . [Is the] center autopilot in command?
PILOT: I don't think so . . . Let me see . . .
CO-PILOT: No . . . The speed is better now.
PILOT: Yeah, shit. Rudder ratio.

CO-PILOT: Yeah . . . I have . . . Let's see, source selector.

The Pilot seeks now to find an alternate static source of input for the cockpit instruments.

PILOT: Yeah, shit. Rudder ratio.
CO-PILOT: Mach trim, mach trim.
PILOT: The speed . . . Let's go to basic instruments. Everything has gone shit.
COCKPIT: [Sound similar to caution alarm, sound similar to alert alarm]
CO-PILOT TO TOWER: Tower, AeroPeru six zero three.
PILOT: We are in emergency.
TOWER: AeroPeru six zero three, Tower, go on.
CO-PILOT TO TOWER: Okay. We declare emergency! We have no basic instruments, no altimeter, no speedometer. We declare an emergency!
TOWER: Roger, altitude?
PILOT: Ahh . . .
CO-PILOT TO TOWER: We don't have, we have until thousand feet . . . Approximately one thousand seven hundred.
PILOT: One thousand, seven hundred.
TOWER: One thousand feet, roger, roger,

AeroPeru six zero three, confirm if you can change frequency one one niner point seven to receive instructions from radar control.
CO-PILOT: We go to one one nine point seven.
PILOT: Auto-throttle has disconnected.
CO-PILOT: Auto-throttle has disconnected.
PILOT: Let's see, what reads there? Let . . .

Pilot asks his Co-pilot to look in the flight manual for information to help them out of their situation. The Co-pilot reads the pertinent data.

CO-PILOT: Auto-throttle disconnect, rudder ratio and mach speed indicator.
PILOT: Okay.
CO-PILOT: Five hundred feet, it's grabbing now . . . These assholes from maintenance move everything.
PILOT: What shit have they done?
CO-PILOT: Auto-throttle, rudder ratio, mach speed trim.
CO-PILOT TO AIR TRAFFIC CONTROL: Let's see if you have us on the radar, Tower, AeroPeru six zero three.
PILOT: I have the command, eh . . . Don't . . .

The Pilot now takes control of the aircraft from the Co-pilot.

AIR TRAFFIC CONTROL LIMA: AeroPeru six oh three, Lima.

PILOT: Autopilots have been connected.

The Pilot sees that the autopilot light is on.

CO-PILOT: No, no, they are disconnected.

PILOT: Ah . . . Are they on?

CO-PILOT: Yes, but they are off, only flight director is on.

CO-PILOT TO ATC: Lima, six zero three.

PILOT TO CO-PILOT: It's maintaining five degrees.

CO-PILOT TO ATC: We request vectors for ILS, Runway Fifteen.

Co-pilot asks for a heading to return to Lima International. Flight 603 starts to turn out to sea, then north along the coast.

PILOT: Not yet, not yet, let's stabilize.

ATC LIMA: Correct, we suggest a right turn heading three three zero.

CO-PILOT TO ATC: Turning right, course three three zero.

ATC LIMA: Affirmative, and keep present altitude.

PILOT: Altitude? We can't . . . We are going up.

CO-PILOT TO ATC: What level [of altitude] do we have? Do we have four thousand feet? Let's see if you confirm us . . .

ATC LIMA: Correct, keeping four thousand.

CO-PILOT TO ATC: We are keeping four thousand.

ATC LIMA: Affirmative.

PILOT: Attitude, just attitude . . . The rudder ratio must be . . . Auto-throttle disconnect.

CO-PILOT: Really . . . We don't have any control.

PILOT: We don't have control, not even the basics.

PILOT: Let's see, check everything.

CO-PILOT: Four thousand feet.

PILOT: Okay, never mind. We keep going up. We are flying without speed. It can't be . . . Let's see . . . Respond.

CO-PILOT: Speed is zero, all speeds.

CO-PILOT TO ATC: We, ah . . . The speed, please, if you have us on the radar?

ATC LIMA: Yes, affirmative, stand by ten seconds. It seems that you are going up with level six zero, at twenty-two miles south, and heading one niner five.

CO-PILOT TO ATC: Okay. That is right. We have course one nine zero and we have seven thousand feet on the altimeter.

ATC LIMA: Yes, correct, now reaching seven zero.

CO-PILOT TO ATC: We have control problems . . .

But Flight 603 did not have control problems. It had instrument problems and problems with indicators like rudder ratio and speed trim signals.

PILOT: Rudder ratio.

ATC LIMA: Okay, roger.

PILOT: Let's see, read rudder ratio and mach trim.

CO-PILOT: Flight controls . . . Rudder ratio . . .

PILOT: Rudder ratio on or not?

CO-PILOT: Yes.

PILOT: Eh . . . Yes.

CO-PILOT: Yes, they are on.

PILOT: Both.

CO-PILOT: Avoid large or abrupt . . .

Co-pilot now starts reading from the flight manual.

PILOT: What?

CO-PILOT: Avoid large or abrupt rudder inputs, if normal left hydraulic system pressure available . . . Left hydraulic system available . . . Yes, crosswind limit. Do not attempt an auto-land, [the manual] says . . .

PILOT: Yeah, bullshit, we can't even fly!

CO-PILOT: I'm trying to set speed . . .

PILOT: But we don't even have . . .

CO-PILOT: Air data.

PILOT: Air data . . . Okay?

CO-PILOT: Alternate air data. I am setting it.

PILOT: Let's see, okay.

CO-PILOT: Nothing. Eight thousand . . . Nine thousand . . . They haven't put us anything.

PILOT: Here it is . . .

ATC LIMA: AeroPeru six oh three, now you show level nine two hundred . . . Ah? What is your course now?

Flight 603 is now over the Pacific, about to head north along the coast.

PILOT: We are flying two hundred.

CO-PILOT TO ATC: Course two zero five.

ATC LIMA: Affirmative, you are turning slowly to the right, correct?

CO-PILOT TO ATC: No, we are keeping course to fly away from the shore.

PILOT: No, we are trying to maintain course . . . We will try to keep ten thousand feet . . . Altitude hold, set it . . . Ten thousand feet.

CO-PILOT: Fast is out now . . . Fast . . . Altitude hold.

ATC LIMA: Your distance is thirty miles. You want course for proceed to localizer, right?

CO-PILOT TO ATC: Correct.

PILOT: Not yet. Let's solve the problem.

ATC LIMA: Turn right, heading three five zero, we suggest . . .

CO-PILOT: But we are going ah . . .

PILOT: Take the autopilots out.

CO-PILOT: Autopilots are out.

PILOT: Yeah, I know.

CO-PILOT: It is leveled now.

PILOT: No . . . Go on.

CO-PILOT: We will set ten thousand feet here in the auto . . .

PILOT: Vertical speed . . . No, no, don't set vert speed hold, hold, altitude hold.

Here the cockpit crew tries to key in new inputs into the command computer.

CO-PILOT: In eleven.

PILOT: Okay, in eleven thousand feet.

CO-PILOT: Twelve, let's put twelve then.

PILOT: Okay. Now it's indicating the speed.

CO-PILOT TO ATC: Okay. We are recovering speed and we request keeping twelve thousand.

PILOT: Flaps . . . Eh . . . Five.

The Pilot realizes that the flaps are still set at 5° from take-off configuration.

COCKPIT: [Sound similar to flap commands moving]

ATC LIMA: Correct, maintain level one two zero. Report starting turn . . . Course to the right. Suggested course three five zero.

CO-PILOT TO ATC: Roger.

PILOT: Decrease power to me. Flap up.

CO-PILOT: Flap up.

COCKPIT: [Sound similar to flap commands moving]

PILOT: Two twenty, we will keep two twenty [mph].

CO-PILOT: Twelve thousand feet.

PILOT: Go on reading [the manual].

CO-PILOT: Nothing else . . . The only thing I made is the air data comp . . .

PILOT: The auto-throttle . . . The autopilot are on.
CO-PILOT: They are not set on.

For the next several seconds the crew experiments with throttle and flap settings.

COCKPIT: [Sound similar to alert]
CO-PILOT: Now we are okay.
PILOT: Yes, now we are okay.
CO-PILOT: Do you want center autopilot?
PILOT: Yeah.

Connecting the autopilot was probably a mistake. The Pilot should have continued to fly the airplane himself.

CO-PILOT: Let's put this.
PILOT: Take the speed out for me.
CO-PILOT: Center autopilot. Pull here.
PILOT: Keep trying.
CO-PILOT: There is no auto-throttle.
PILOT: The speed . . . Autopilot off.
CO-PILOT: Airspeed . . . Autopilot off.
PILOT: At two twenty we will keep manual [controls].
CO-PILOT: Okay.
ATC LIMA: AeroPeru six zero three, you are forty miles from Lima and according with information on screen at level one two zero [12,000 feet] approximate speed over the ground is three hundred and ten knots [357 mph].
PILOT: Roger . . .
CO-PILOT TO ATC: Roger . . . We have two thirty and are turning to course three thirty.
ATC LIMA: Okay. Roger.
CO-PILOT: Rudder ratio follows . . . Mach speed trim.
PILOT: Okay. Let's see ah . . . Read all that . . . Auto-throttle is connect, command, one two zero feet here, correct?
CO-PILOT: Twelve thousand feet.

Again, the crew relies on the autopilot.

CO-PILOT: Ah . . . Auto-flight, now what? Auto-throttle, rudder ratio, I read it already . . . Mach speed trim, mach speed is in navigation, flight instruments, flight instruments, auto-flight, auto-flight, altitude alert, autopilot disconnect, rudder ratio, okay.
PILOT: Hey, shit, we are going down now! Hey, shit, this auto-throttle . . . The autopilot is fuck off!
CO-PILOT: Speed, altitude alert, autopilot disconnect . . .

PILOT: Three thirty.

CO-PILOT: . . . Autopilot inoperative, flight instruments switch, mach speed, I don't find that mach speed trim . . . Speed, we have speed problems, instrument source selector, flight director.

PILOT: It can't be. Hey, the speed. Look. The power we have . . . It can't be!

CO-PILOT: It can't be, it's true, it's wrong . . . Three thirty [knots].

PILOT: Yes, but they are even, aren't they?

CO-PILOT: Okay, set yours on alternate air data, the one down there, the lower button. Oh, shit. Worse. Your altimeter goes to shit!

PILOT: Fuck. Basic instruments, let's go to basic instruments!

CO-PILOT: Basic instruments.

PILOT: Eh . . . The air data gone shit there.

CO-PILOT: I'll fill here the departure and arrival . . . ILS Runway Fifteen . . . Insert.

Now, the Co-pilot keys in data to the computer needed for landing.

PILOT: Okay. Yours is screwed up . . . The air data.

CO-PILOT: Two four eight, two four eight, nineteen seven.

PILOT: We are with three three zero [heading].

CO-PILOT: With three thirty.

ATC LIMA: AeroPeru six zero three, you are at forty miles, correct? Flying parallel course three three zero. You are flying left [of] course about to intersect west of Lima.

CO-PILOT: It is falling . . .

CO-PILOT TO ATC: Correct, we request vectors from this moment on.

PILOT: We are going to stabilize and . . . Let's see . . .

ATC LIMA: Roger, we suggest course three six zero.

CO-PILOT TO ATC: Three six zero.

ATC LIMA: The Lima VOR, do you receive it okay?

CO-PILOT TO ATC Affirmative.

PILOT: There is no flight director [autopilot] . . . No auto-throttle either . . . And where . . . Where. Is this going up?

COCKPIT: [Sound similar to engines accelerating]

CO-PILOT TO ATC: Okay. I understand, for . . . three one five, turn right to intercept localizer. Ah . . . We still don't have . . . Ah . . .

PILOT: Auto-throttle off. Hey, you know, it's . . .

CO-PILOT: It's falling!

PILOT: Shit, yeah!

CO-PILOT: [Airspeed is] going up too much.

PILOT: It doesn't dis . . . Apparently doesn't disconnect the auto . . .

COCKPIT: [Sound similar to alert]

CO-PILOT: Autopilot disconnected, better if we control it on basics, isn't it?

PILOT: Let's see the trim.

ATC LIMA: According to presentation [on radar] you are crossing radial two three zero from Lima, distance west southwest is thirty-seven miles.

CO-PILOT TO ATC: Correct . . . We will . . . We have problems here for reading instruments. You will have to help us in altitudes and speed if possible.

ATC LIMA: Okay, roger.

CO-PILOT TO ATC: Until we reach the localizer beam and we will navigate some three zero miles north of the localizer of Lima VOR to center in the ILS.

PILOT: It doesn't have alt[itude] hold . . . Set the approach, please.

CO-PILOT: I did it, I did it.

PILOT: Then let's go.

CO-PILOT: Okay the approach . . .

PILOT: Let's see, we will try to go down. Okay with this course and . . . Why it doesn't appear . . . Ah . . . Okay, okay. I'll try to go down with everything cut . . . Ah . . . Okay.

CO-PILOT: [The speed is] going up.

PILOT: Let's go down to ten thousand feet . . . Why does speed gets so high? Is it the real speed?

CO-PILOT: This is what worries me . . . No, I don't think so . . .

PILOT: It can't be . . . Then . . . Rudder ratio, mach trim . . . Then if there is not that . . . Mach speed trim?

CO-PILOT: No, there is no mach speed trim . . . I don't find . . . Let's see, keep flying it. It will . . .

CO-PILOT TO ATC: Can you tell us the speed, please?

ATC LIMA: It indicates three two zero [320 knots].

CO-PILOT TO ATC: Correct, we have all engines cut and it's accelerating . . . Accelerating.

CO-PILOT: Take the speed brake out.

PILOT: No . . . Eh . . . No. Let's see, maybe . . . Let's see, take out . . .

CO-PILOT: Speed is okay. All three indicators are okay in speed . . . Fast, fast. All engine instruments are okay, all engine instruments are okay. Shit!

PILOT: What would be the real speed?

CO-PILOT: This one is okay. They are okay, the speed . . . Airspeed . . .

PILOT: But with all power cut down, it can't be, with all cut down . . . There's a problem with the source instrument. Let's see, how many miles . . . At thirty miles from Lima, we start descending with spoilers and flight level change.

ATC LIMA: You are crossing the two six zero of Lima, at thirty-one miles west. Flight level is one hundred plus seven hundred, and approximate speed is two eight zero over the ground.

PILOT: Yeah . . . Perfect.

CO-PILOT TO ATC: Yeah, but we have an indication of three hundred fifty knots here.

PILOT: Let's put. Why are these more clear?

COCKPIT: [A two-tone over speed alarm sounds]

PILOT: Overspeed. Fucking shit! I have speed brakes. Everything has gone, all instruments went to shit. Everything has gone. All of them . . .

The Captain had deployed the air brakes, but the instruments do not show the airplane slowing down. Rather, they show an increase *in speed, while the aircraft in fact has slowed to near stall speed. The overspeed warning is sounding in his ears while the stick shaker on the control yoke is telling him that he is in a stall.*

COCKPIT: [Sound of stall warning alarm]

CO-PILOT: We are going down!

PILOT: Ah . . .

CO-PILOT: I don't think so . . . It can't be overspeed.

COCKPIT: [Sound of stall warning alarms]

CO-PILOT: We are flying . . . Looing of . . .

COCKPIT: [Sound of stall warning alarm]

CO-PILOT TO ATC: Is there any possibilities of . . .

COCKPIT: [Sound of stall warning alarm]

CO-PILOT TO ATC: We still have overspeed.

PILOT: But with spoilers . . . All of the . . .

ATC LIMA: Correct, rescue has been warned . . .

CO-PILOT TO ATC: We request . . . Is there any airplane that can take off to rescue us?

PILOT: Eh? . . . Wait, no, no, no, no.

ATC LIMA: Yes, correct. We are going to

coordinate immediately. It's being coordinated immediately.

CO-PILOT TO ATC: Any plane that can guide us, an AeroPeru that may be around? Somebody?

PILOT: Don't tell him anything about that!

CO-PILOT: Yes, because right now we are stalling . . .

ATC LIMA: Attention, we have a [Boeing] seven oh seven that will depart . . . We are telling him.

PILOT: We are not stalling! It's fictitious, it's fictitious.

The speedometers indicate overspeed, which the Pilot believes to be true. Meanwhile the airbrakes are stalling the airplane. The Captain had two choices, and he chose to believe what the instruments were telling him, unaware that the instruments were unable to give a reading that was accurate. The Co-pilot, on the other hand, believes what the stick shaker tells him – that they are in a stall.

CO-PILOT: No! If we have shaker how would it be not . . .

PILOT: Shaker . . . But it is . . . Eh . . . But even with speed brakes on we are maintaining nine thousand five hundred . . . Why do we read the same . . . ? I don't understand . . . Power. What power do we have?

The Pilot continues to believe his instruments – now in his altimeter. But their throttle settings do not coincide with the speed that their instruments are indicating – 454 mph.

CO-PILOT: It's coming back, look . . . My speedometer is coming back.

PILOT: No, it has gone to off.

CO-PILOT: It has gone to off.

ATC LIMA: AeroPeru six zero three, you have turned slightly to the left. Now you are heading three two zero and your level is one hundred, approximate speed of two two zero knots and a distance of thirty-two miles northwest of Lima.

COCKPIT: [Sound similar to double alert alarm]

CO-PILOT: You are going down! . . . Eh . . . One zero zero to runway, look! Let's program. I think . . . Eh . . .

CO-PILOT TO ATC: We have a problem here . . .

CO-PILOT: Overspeed . . . It doesn't cut . . .

The overspeed . . . Where is the overspeed! Where is the overspeed warning, shit!

PILOT: Nine thousand feet if it indicates you . . . It's fictitious. Everything is fictitious. The air data has gone to shit.

ATC LIMA: AeroPeru six zero three, your base is [asking] if you have both computer systems out of service.

CO-PILOT TO ATC: We have . . . No instrument is working as speedometer, we have overspeed alarm and no . . . Apparently it is not . . . Having overspeed shaker . . . The fast forward is indicating too high speed. We have engines cut down and [it] doesn't decelerate apparently . . .

PILOT: Apparently.

CO-PILOT: Let's see. Accelerate one engine . . . No, it ejects it back.

PILOT: Because the auto-throttle is on.

CO-PILOT: Auto-throttle off. Let's see . . . Accelerate!

ATC LIMA: The seven oh seven will be ready in some fifteen minutes to fly west in your help.

COCKPIT: [Sound of mechanical alert] *Too low terrain.*

PILOT: What happened?

CO-PILOT: Too low terrain.

The crew could have referred to radio altimeters which do not depend on the static ports. However, they chose to rely on the altimeters that required the static ports, thereby worsening their predicament.

PILOT: But . . . Let's go left.

The Pilot assumes that they are flying over the ground, rather than over water.

CO-PILOT TO ATC: We have terrain alarm, we have terrain alarm!

COCKPIT: [Sound of wind shear warning] *Too low terrain.*

ATC LIMA: Roger, according to monitor . . . It indicates flight level one zero zero, over the sea, heading a northwest course of three zero zero.

CO-PILOT TO ATC: We have terrain alarm and we are supposed to be at ten thousand feet?

PILOT: Shit, we have everything.

COCKPIT: [Sound of wind shear warning]

ATC LIMA: According to monitor you have one zero five.

CO-PILOT TO ATC: We have all computers crazy here . . .

PILOT: Shit, what the hell these assholes have done.

ATC LIMA: Roger, AeroPeru six zero three, it shows that you are turning left, you are aiming to the west [out to sea].

CO-PILOT TO ATC: I don't understand.

ATC LIMA: It shows that you are turning left, you are aiming to the west.

CO-PILOT TO ATC: Affirmative, we are heading two five zero, but we are going over the sea because we have low terrain alarm . . .

PILOT: We are going to the sea.

ATC LIMA: Yes, affirmative. It shows that you are at forty-two miles, flying with course west, course two five zero heading west . . .

CO-PILOT TO ATC: We are over water, aren't we?

ATC LIMA: Affirmative, over the water, you are forty-two miles west.

CO-PILOT TO ATC: Okay.

PILOT: Are we going down now?

CO-PILOT TO ATC: We don't have . . . We have, like, three seven zero knots. Are we descending now?

ATC LIMA: It shows the same speed . . . You have two zero zero speed approximately.

CO-PILOT TO ATC: Two zero zero of speed?

ATC LIMA: Two two zero of speed over the ground, reducing speed slightly.

PILOT: Shit! We will stall now . . .

COCKPIT: [Sound of sink rate alarm]

A steep descent activates the sink rate alarm.

CO-PILOT: Let's go up, let's see. Let's go up here.

Aircraft climbs to 2,400, descends to 1,300, then climbs again to 4,000 feet. But the altimeters show them at 9,000. The crew believe they are flying at 10,000 feet.

CO-PILOT: Overspeed. This shit.

PILOT: The overspeed no, this . . . eh . . . Cabin altitude alert, mach, now we must . . .

CO-PILOT: Shit.

PILOT: Eh . . . Read one by one, I'll fly here . . . And forty-five miles . . . You read. You make the emergency.

CO-PILOT: Overspeed . . . Fuck . . . Go higher.

PILOT: These sons of a bitch.

CO-PILOT: Your speaker, let's see . . . Overspeed again. I don't have overspeed . . .

I don't have overspeed . . . Auto-throttle, cabin altitude inoperative.

ATC LIMA: AeroPeru six zero three, you are at fifty miles from Lima flying west, course two seven zero, with level one hundred.

PILOT: Okay . . . Let's go back, let's set course hundred . . . Hundred . . .

Now the Captain sets a course to return to Lima, and begins to prepare the aircraft for descent and landing.

CO-PILOT TO ATC: Ah . . . Affirmative, we are setting course three six zero.

ATC LIMA: Okay. Roger, correct.

CO-PILOT TO ATC: Ah . . . Do you have [our] speed?

ATC LIMA: Yes, it shows a speed of approximately three zero zero knots.

CO-PILOT TO ATC: What about some plane that can give us [altitude and speed indications]?

ATC LIMA: Correct. A Boeing seven oh seven has been coordinated. It will be ready in about fifteen minutes, the Tower informed some minutes ago.

CO-PILOT: Autopilot, overspeed, I don't find overspeed.

Co-pilot is looking in the Boeing operating manual for overspeed instructions.

PILOT: How do we know the speed we have?

CO-PILOT: Fast, fast. Horizons are okay . . . Horizons are right. It's the only thing that is right.

PILOT: Flight level change.

CO-PILOT [reading from manual]: Apu, engines, auto-flight, apu engines, auto-flight instruments, cargo fire, ditching, emergency equipment, passenger evacuation, electrical, flight controls, fuel, hydraulic, ice and rain, landing gear, flight instruments, auto-throttle disconnect . . . Let's see if we put the . . .

PILOT: Cabin alt[itude] inoperative.

CO-PILOT: Yeah, never mind. Let's put in manual to go down manual. Zero ten. That's it. Auto disconnect . . . three nine zero knots, says here, eh . . . On the airspeed indicator. I'll try to intercept the ILS. I'm trying to go down.

CO-PILOT TO ATC: Lima, AeroPeru six zero three, we will try to intercept the ILS. Let's see if you tell us if we are in . . .

COCKPIT: [Sound similar to caution alarm]

ATC LIMA: Roger, AeroPeru six zero three, you show now level nine seven hundred.

CO-PILOT: That is right.

ATC LIMA: Stand by to verify speed. The [Boeing] seven oh seven is about to take off. It is starting to move.

PILOT: This is . . . Fuck off.

CO-PILOT TO ATC: Verify the speed. It is very important. We don't have speed on board.

ATC LIMA: Correct. You are starting turn and it shows a velocity of two seven zero ground speed.

CO-PILOT TO PILOT: Not so much, there it is. Two seven zero is fine.

The Co-pilot is asking the Captain not to increase the speed.

PILOT: Alerts, altitude alerts.

CO-PILOT: Altitude, autopilot. Don't put any autopilot, Captain . . . Alt alert, autopilot disconnect . . .

PILOT: Let's go to . . .

CO-PILOT: Autopilot disconnect, zero six zero three.

PILOT: Ask him to tell us . . .

CO-PILOT [reading from manual]: Autopilot disconnect . . . Crew awareness. Nothing else says . . . Autopilot inoperative, auto throttle disconnect . . . Crew awareness. Alt, alert, cabin inoperative, rudder ratio, there is nothing new . . . But the overspeed . . .

ATC LIMA: Course to intercept localizer. Approximately at thirty miles. You must fly heading zero seven zero approximately. Keep the course stable . . .

CO-PILOT: Yes, turn now . . . Zero seventy.

CO-PILOT TO ATC: We will keep zero seventy. We keep course. It seems that we have the right course. What we don't have is airspeed indicator and altitude nine seven-hundred feet.

PILOT: Flight level change.

ATC LIMA: Correct. Altitude is nine seven hundred. And the speed is two four zero knots over the ground, according to monitor.

COCKPIT: [Sound similar to warning alarm]

CO-PILOT: What if we put [down] flaps? . . . Two hundred forty.

PILOT: What?

CO-PILOT: If we put [down] flaps?

ATC LIMA: . . . And at fifty-one miles from Lima.

PILOT: Okay.

CO-PILOT: Zero seventy . . . I want to take that shit out of there!

PILOT: The overspeed? . . . But you can't.

COCKPIT: [Alarm warning]

CO-PILOT: You can't?

PILOT: Let's see . . . You, switch your thing . . .

CO-PILOT: Air data? . . . No . . . But it's flying well, I have the . . . If not, I'm going . . . Shit.

PILOT: How can it be flying at this speed if we are going down with all the power cut off?

CO-PILOT TO ATC Can you tell me the altitude please, because we have the climb that doesn't . . .

PILOT: Nine.

COCKPIT: [Alarm warning of too low terrain]

ATC LIMA: Yes, you keep nine seven hundred [9,700 feet] according to presentation [on radar], sir.

CO-PILOT TO ATC: Nine seven hundred?

ATC LIMA: Yes, correct. What is the indicated altitude on board? Have you any visual reference?

CO-PILOT TO ATC: Nine seven hundred, but it indicates too low terrain . . . Are you sure that you have us on the radar at fifty miles?

PILOT: Hey, look . . . With three seven zero we have . . .

CO-PILOT: Have what? Three seven zero of what? Do we lower the gear?

PILOT: But, what do we do with the gear? Don't know . . . that.

COCKPIT: [Sound of initial impact with the water]

CO-PILOT TO ATC: We are impacting water!! Pull it up!!

ATC LIMA: Go up, go up if it indicates pull up.

PILOT: I have it, I have it!

COCKPIT: [Warning sound for too low terrain]

PILOT: We are going to invert! [Turn upside down]

COCKPIT: [Sound of alarms] *Whoop . . . Whoop . . . Pull . . .*

COCKPIT: [Sound of impact]

END OF TAPE

At impact with the water the onboard altimeters indicated an altitude of 9,700 feet. The aircraft's left wing and engine made initial contact with the water at a 10° angle, at 300 mph. The aircraft then climbed 200 feet, turned over and fell again, crashing into the sea. The wreckage was subsequently recovered. All souls aboard were lost.

3 BAN NONG WAENG, Thailand
26 May 1991

This CVR transcript documents a freak accident. No piloting skills could have saved the 213 passengers and the crew of ten that night aboard the Lauda Air Flight 004, a Boeing 767, named the *Mozart*, out of Bangkok International Airport, bound for Vienna's Wien-Schwechat. The passengers were mostly Austrian, German, Swiss and Hong Kong Chinese. Many of them were returning from holidays in Thailand; some were travelling on business.

The flight, which had originated in Hong Kong, took off from Bangkok at 11.10 p.m. Twelve minutes later, the crew got a visual advisory warning on its annunciator panel that a system failure might cause the in-flight deployment of the No. 1 engine's thrust reverser, which brakes the aircraft on the ground by throwing the thrust of the jet engines forward of the wing through the mechanism of mechanical scoops. A deployment in-flight of the thrust reverser is by definition catastrophic. It is almost unthinkable.

The crew assumed that the annunciator warning was a false reading caused by moisture in the system. The crew could not have seriously believed that the thrust reversers would activate in-flight, no matter what. Besides, Boeing 767's Emergency/Malfunction Checklist, to which the crew referred right away, reported 'No action required'.

Nine minutes after the advisory, 21 minutes into the flight, the No. 1 thrust reverser deployed. The Boeing disintegrated at 4,000 feet.

We pick up the CVR just as the Captain receives the notification of 'an additional system failure [which] might cause inflight deployment of the thrust reverser'. This was the first and only warning.

CAPTAIN: Shit. That keeps . . . that's coming on.
CO-PILOT: So we passed transition altitude one-zero-one-three.
CAPTAIN: Okay. What's it say in there about that [deployment in-flight of thrust reverser], just ah . . .
CO-PILOT Reads from Boeing 767 manual:

Additional system failures may cause in-flight deployment. Expect normal reverse operation after landing.

CAPTAIN: Okay. Just, ah, let's see. Okay.

CO-PILOT: Shall I ask the ground staff?

CAPTAIN: What's that?

CO-PILOT: Shall I ask the technical men [on the ground]?

CAPTAIN: Ah, you can tell 'em it, just it's, it's, it's, just – ah, no, ah, it's probably, ah, well . . . ah, moisture or something 'cause it's not just, oh, it's [the annunciator panel light] coming on and off.

CO-PILOT: Yeah.

CAPTAIN: But, ah, you know it's a . . . it doesn't really, it's just an advisory thing, I don't, ah . . . Could be some moisture in there or somethin'.

CO-PILOT: [I] think you need a little bit of rudder trim to the left.

CAPTAIN: What's that?

CO-PILOT: You need a little bit of rudder trim to the left. [He starts adding up figures in German.]

CAPTAIN [Apparently sees instruments]: Ah, reverser's deployed.

COCKPIT: [Sound of snap]

CAPTAIN: Jesus Christ!

COCKPIT: [Sound of four caution tones, sound of siren warning starts, stops, starts again and continues until the recording ends]

CAPTAIN: Here, wait a minute! Damn it!

COCKPIT: [Sound of bang]

END OF TAPE

Lauda Air Flight 004 disintegrated at an elevation of nearly 4,000 feet; the fuselage crashed in the Thai jungle at a 45° angle. One of the aircraft's wings was found more than a mile from the main crash site; the cockpit was found just over a mile from the main crash site. The probable cause of the crash was the in-flight deployment of the No. 1 engine thrust reverser, which itself was caused by a failure of the thrust reverser isolation valve. The official report determined that '. . . recovery from the event was uncontrollable [sic] for an unexpecting flight crew.' All souls aboard were lost.

That morning in clear California skies, Pacific Southwest Airline's Flight 182, a Boeing 727–214 with seven crew members and 128 passengers, was making its approach into San Diego's Lindbergh Field after a short flight that had originated at Los Angeles International Airport. The approach was visual to Runway 27, over the office towers on the hills of San Diego that overlook the harbour.

The PSA crew was aware of other airplane traffic in the area, including the presence of a small, single-engined Cessna 172, which had taken off at 08.16 from nearby Montgomery Field and had proceeded to Lindbergh Field, where it had already practised two instrument landings. At 09.00 the Cessna pilot was instructed to maintain Visual Flight Rules at or below 3,500 feet, heading 70°. At that moment, PSA Flight 182 was flying over San Diego at 2,600 feet.

We pick up the CVR tape just as the PSA cockpit is being notified of traffic in the area.

APPROACH CONTROL: PSA one eighty-two, traffic [at] twelve o'clock, one mile northbound.

CAPTAIN: We're looking.

APPROACH: PSA one eighty-two, additional traffic's, ah, twelve o'clock, three miles just north of the field northwestbound, a Cessna one seventy-two climbing VFR [Visual Flight Rules] out of one thousand four hundred [feet].

CO-PILOT: Okay, we've got that other [at] twelve [o'clock].

APPROACH TO THE CESSNA 172: Cessna seven seven one one golf, San Diego departure radar contact, maintain VFR conditions at or below three thousand five hundred, fly heading zero seven zero, vector final approach course . . .

APPROACH: PSA one eighty-two, traffic's at twelve o'clock, three miles out of one thousand seven hundred.

CO-PILOT: Got 'em.

CAPTAIN: Traffic in sight.

APPROACH: Okay, sir, maintain visual separation, contact Lindbergh tower one three three point three, have a nice day now.

CAPTAIN: Okay.

CAPTAIN: Lindbergh PSA one eighty-two downwind.

TOWER: PSA one eighty-two, Lindbergh tower, ah, traffic twelve o'clock one mile a Cessna.

CO-PILOT TO CAPTAIN: Flaps five.

CAPTAIN: Is that the one [the traffic] we're looking at?

CO-PILOT: Yeah, but I don't see him now.

CAPTAIN: Okay, we had it there a minute ago.

TOWER: One eighty-two, roger.

CAPTAIN: I think he's [the traffic] pass[ed] to our right.

TOWER: Yeah.

CAPTAIN: He was right over here a minute ago.

TOWER: How far are you going to take your downwind? Company traffic is waiting for departure.

CAPTAIN: Ah, probably about three to four miles.

TOWER: Okay. PSA one eighty-two, cleared to land.

CAPTAIN: One eighty-two's cleared to land.

CO-PILOT: Are we clear of that Cessna?

FLIGHT ENGINEER: Suppose to be.

CAPTAIN: I guess.

A PSA CAPTAIN WHO WAS STANDING IN COCKPIT OBSERVING: I hope.

CAPTAIN: Oh yeah, before we turned downwind, I saw him about one o'clock, [he's] probably behind us now.

CO-PILOT: There's one [an airplane] underneath [us]. I was looking at that inbound there.

CAPTAIN: Whoop!

CO-PILOT: Aghhh!

CABIN: [Sound of impact with the Cessna in mid-air]

CAPTAIN: Easy baby, easy baby. What have we got here?

CO-PILOT: It's bad. We're hit man, we are hit.

CAPTAIN: Tower, we're going down, this is PSA . . .

TOWER: Okay, we'll call the equipment for you.

CABIN: [Sound of stall warning]

END OF TAPE

After collision with the Cessna, the PSA plummeted to the ground into a residential area of San Diego. All 135 passengers and crew of the PSA died; nine souls on the ground were also killed.

The story of Korean Air Lines 007 (KAL 007) is by now part of the dark legend of the Cold War. Mistaken as a US spy airplane, the Korean Airlines Boeing 747, which was flying well off course into restricted Soviet airspace, was approached and shot down by an intercepting MIG pilot, who had sighted the KAL and fired a heat-seeking missile at its fuselage. Out of control, KAL plunged to the ocean below, where its black box was recovered weeks later.

We pick up the transcript seconds before the missile struck the airplane and follow the transcript for roughly seven minutes as the Boeing 747 plunged 35,000 feet into the sea.

TOKYO AIR TRAFFIC CONTROL: Korean Air zero zero seven clearance, Tokyo ATC clears Korean Air zero zero seven [to] climb and maintain flight level three five zero [35,000 feet].

CAPTAIN: Ah, roger, Korean Air zero zero seven, climb and maintain at three five zero, leaving three three zero at this time [33,000 feet].

TOKYO ATC: Tokyo roger.

COCKPIT: [Sound of altitude alert]

CAPTAIN: Tokyo radio, Korean Air zero zero seven reaching level three five zero [35,000 feet].

TOKYO ATC: Korean Air zero zero seven, Tokyo roger.

COCKPIT: [Sound of explosion]

CAPTAIN: What's happened?

CO-PILOT: What?

CAPTAIN: Retard throttles.

CO-PILOT: Engines normal.

CAPTAIN: Landing gear.

COCKPIT: [Sound of cabin altitude warning]

CAPTAIN: Landing gear.

COCKPIT: [Sound of altitude deviation warning, sound of autopilot disconnect warning]

CAPTAIN: Altitude is going up. Altitude is going up. Speed brake is coming out.

CO-PILOT: What? What?

CAPTAIN: Check it out.

COCKPIT: [Sound of Public Address chime for automatic cabin announcement]

CO-PILOT: I am not able to drop altitude; now unable.

PUBLIC ADDRESS RECORDING: Attention, emergency descent.

CAPTAIN: Altitude is going up. This is not working. This is not working. Manually.

CO-PILOT: Cannot do manually.

COCKPIT: Attention emergency descent [in Japanese.] [Sound of autopilot disconnect warning]

CO-PILOT: Not working manually also. Engines are normal, sir.

PUBLIC ADDRESS RECORDING: Put out your cigarette. This is an emergency descent. Put out your cigarette. This is an emergency descent.

CAPTAIN: Is it power compression?

FLIGHT ENGINEER: Is that right?

PUBLIC ADDRESS RECORDING: Put out your cigarette. This is an emergency descent.

FLIGHT ENGINEER: All of both . . .

CAPTAIN: Is that right?

PUBLIC ADDRESS RECORDING: Put the mask over your nose and mouth and adjust the headband.

CO-PILOT: Tokyo radio Korean Air zero zero seven.

PUBLIC ADDRESS RECORDING: Put the mask over your nose and mouth and adjust the headband.

TOKYO ATC: Korean Air zero zero seven, Tokyo.

CO-PILOT: Roger, Korean Air zero zero seven . . . ah, we are experiencing . . .

PUBLIC ADDRESS RECORDING: Put the mask over your nose and mouth and adjust the headband.

FLIGHT ENGINEER: All compression.

CAPTAIN: Rapid decompression. Descend to one zero thousand [10,000 feet].

PUBLIC ADDRESS RECORDING: Attention, emergency descent. Attention emergency descent.

FLIGHT ENGINEER: Now . . . we have to set this.

TOKYO ATC: Korean Air zero zero seven, radio check on one zero zero four eight.

PUBLIC ADDRESS RECORDING: Attention emergency descent.

FLIGHT ENGINEER: Speed. Stand by. Stand by. Stand by. Stand by. Set.

PUBLIC ADDRESS RECORDING: Put out your cigarette. This is an emergency descent. Put out your cigarette. This is an emergency descent. Put out your cigarette. This is an emergency descent. Put the mask over your

nose and mouth and adjust the headband.
Put the mask over your nose and mouth
and adjust . . .

END OF TAPE

All souls aboard were lost.

As much as anything else, South African Airways Boeing 747–244B, registered as Flight 295, which was carrying 140 passengers and a crew of 19, shows the confusion that can overcome a cockpit crew when confronted with an emergency – in this instance, a catastrophic cargo-hold fire.

Flight 295 took off from Chiang Kai Shek airport in Taiwan that afternoon, bound for South Africa. Just before midnight, while flying over the southern Indian Ocean, the crew reported a fire in one of the six cargo pallets in the main air-freight hold. The Boeing 747 made an emergency descent, and Mauritius Air Traffic Control gave the flight an approach clearance.

We pick up the CVR transcript just as the cockpit crew notifies Mauritius Approach of a fire on board, and asks for permission to descend to 14,000 feet.

CAPTAIN TO MAURITIUS APPROACH: Er, good morning. We have, er, a smoke problem and we are doing an emergency descent to level one five, er, one four zero [14,000 feet].

MAURITIUS APPROACH: Confirm you wish to descend to flight level one four zero [14,000 feet]?

CAPTAIN: Ja, we have already commenced, er, due to a smoke problem in the airplane.

APPROACH: Eh, roger. You are clear to descend immediately to flight level one four zero.

CAPTAIN: Roger, we will appreciate it if you can alert, er, fire, er, er, er.

APPROACH: Do you request a full emergency please? A full emergency?

CAPTAIN: Affirmative, that's Charlie, Charlie.

APPROACH: Roger, I declare a full emergency.

CAPTAIN: Thank you.

APPROACH: [Asks the aircraft crew for a position report]

CAPTAIN: Now we have lost a lot of electrics. We haven't got any [lights] on the aircraft now.

APPROACH: [Asks for an Estimated Time of Arrival and an update of the aircraft's position. Advises that both runways are available]

CAPTAIN: Er, we'd like to track in er, one, er, one three [Runway 13].

APPROACH: Confirm Runway Thirteen?

CAPTAIN: Charlie, Charlie [yes, yes].

COCKPIT: [Fire alarm bell sounds, followed by public address system chime]

FLIGHT ENGINEER: What's going on now . . . Cargo? It came on now afterwards. Main deck cargo . . . then the other one came on as well. I've got two.

CAPTAIN: [Calls for checklist to be read.] It is the fact that both came on. It disturbs one.

VOICE IN COCKPIT: Aagh!

CAPTAIN: What's going on now?

COCKPIT: [Sudden bang]

END OF TAPE

The probable cause of the crash was a fire of an unknown origin that had possibly: 1) incapacitated the crew; 2) caused disorientation of the crew due to thick smoke; 3) caused crew distraction; 4) weakened the aircraft structure, causing an in-flight break-up; 5) burned through several control cables; 6) caused loss of control due to deformation of the aircraft fuselage. All souls aboard were lost.

This disaster has been much analyzed for what the cockpit crew did and did not do in a timely fashion.

The Captain of Avianca Flight 052, a Boeing 707 which had originated in Medellin, Colombia, bound for New York's JFK airport, had repeatedly asked his co-pilot to declare a 'fuel emergency' with the air traffic controllers at JFK airport. The fuel aboard the 707 was inexplicably low upon arrival in the New York City area. The flight crew, long aware of the fuel situation, had tried to maximize the efficiency of the fuel pumps, so that the last few drops of jet fuel in the tanks would reach the four Pratt & Whitney engines. A declaration of a fuel emergency to the New York Approach or the Kennedy Tower would have given Flight 052 priority over all other aircraft and, without a doubt, would have taken Flight 052 out of harm's way. Without a declaration of an emergency, with the Approach Controllers unaware of their urgent need to land, Flight 052 circled JFK for nearly an hour. The Captain was flying the aircraft, with the Co-pilot communicating with New York Approach and the tower. The time was around 9 p.m.

CO-PILOT: New York Approach Avianca zero five two levelling five thousand [feet].

NY APPROACH: Avianca zero five two heavy, New York Approach, good evening. Fly heading zero six zero.

CO-PILOT: Heading zero six zero, Avianca zero five two heavy.

FLIGHT ENGINEER: When we have . . . a thousand pounds or less in any tank. It is necessary to do [an emergency landing].

CO-PILOT: Yes, sir.

ENGINEER: The Go Around procedure is stating that the power be applied slowly and to avoid rapid accelerations and to have a minimum of nose up attitude.

CAPTAIN: To maintain what?

CO-PILOT: Minimum, minimum nose up attitude. That means the less nose-up attitude that one can hold.

ENGINEER: This thing is going okay.

CO-PILOT: Then flaps to twenty-five position and maintain Vee ref plus twenty . . . The highest go around procedure is starting.

ENGINEER [reading from flight manual]: The flaps, sorry, retract the landing gear with positive rate of climb . . . if any low pressure light comes on do not select the switch in the off position . . . The low pressure lights of the [fuel] pumps comes on. Reduce the nose up attitude, the nose up attitude.

CO-PILOT: The forward [fuel] pumps . . .

captain: What heading do you have over there? Select Kennedy on my side.

CO-PILOT: Kennedy is on the number two, but if [you] want, Commander, I can perform the radio setup right now that we are now being vectored. We are like on downwind position now.

CAPTAIN: We passed [the airport] already, no?

CO-PILOT: Yes sir.

NY APPROACH: Avianca zero five two heavy turn left, heading three six zero.

CO-PILOT: Left, heading three six zero, Avianca zero five two heavy.

ENGINEER: Three six zero.

CO-PILOT: Yes, Commander, that's what he says.

CAPTAIN: Perform the radio setup, but leave to me the VOR . . . Two what?

CO-PILOT: Two twenty-three.

CAPTAIN: Two twenty-three. What heading he provide us?

CO-PILOT: New. He give us three six zero.

CAPTAIN: Okay.

CO-PILOT: I am going to perform the radio setup on number two.

CAPTAIN: Perform the radio setup.

COCKPIT: [Sound of landing gear warning horn]

CAPTAIN: Hey, [I] understand that the nose must be maintained as low as possible, yes?

ENGINEER: That's correct. It says that the forward pumps . . .

The Flight Engineer is trying to keep fuel supplied to the engines. The 'pumps' he is talking about are pumping fuel into the engines.

NY APPROACH: Avianca zero five two heavy, turn left heading of three zero zero.

CO-PILOT TO APPROACH: Left heading three zero zero, Avianca zero five two heavy. Three zero zero on the heading.

ENGINEER: The forward boost pumps could be uncovered on fuel during the go around.

What it means, it doesn't contain fuel for feeding itself and a flameout can occur [in other words, the pumps may have no fuel to pump] . . . and it is necessary to lower the nose again [to get fuel into the pumps].

CAPTAIN: Heading three hundred.

CO-PILOT: Three hundred. Right now we are proceeding to the airport inbound and we have twenty-seven, seventeen miles.

ENGINEER: Roger.

CO-PILOT: This means that we'll have hamburger tonight.

NY APPROACH: Avianca zero five two heavy, turn left heading two niner.

CO-PILOT: Left heading two niner zero, Avianca zero five two heavy. Two niner zero on the heading please.

CAPTAIN: Two twenty-three course counter standby the frequency number.

CO-PILOT: Standby for the frequency.

CAPTAIN: Leave the ILS frequency in Kennedy until I advise you. Select your own there.

CO-PILOT: It is ready.

CAPTAIN: Well . . .

CO-PILOT: Markers are set.

NY APPROACH: Avianca zero five two heavy, descend and maintain, ah, descend and maintain three thousand [feet].

CO-PILOT: Descend and maintain three thousand, Avianca zero five two heavy.

ENGINEER: They got us. They [are] already vectoring us.

CO-PILOT: They accommodate [letting us land] us ahead of an . . .

CAPTAIN: What?

CO-PILOT: They accommodate us.

ENGINEER: They already know that we are in bad condition.

CAPTAIN: No, they are descending us.

CO-PILOT: One thousand feet.

CAPTAIN: Ah, yes.

CO-PILOT: They are giving us priority.

NY APPROACH: Avianca zero five two heavy, turn left heading two seven zero.

CO-PILOT: Left heading two seven zero.

CO-PILOT: Two seven zero on the heading.

CAPTAIN: Two seventy.

CO-PILOT: [The runway] is ahead of us.

ENGINEER: Yes.

CAPTAIN: Standby for the localizer there.

CO-PILOT: Yes, sir. Outer marker is seven miles.

NY APPROACH: Avianca zero five two heavy, turn left heading two five zero, intercept the localizer.

CO-PILOT: Heading two five zero, intercept the localizer, Avianca zero five two heavy.

This is final vector. Do you want the ILS, Commander?

NY APPROACH: Avianca zero five two heavy, you are one five miles from the outer marker. Maintain two thousand [feet] until established on the localizer. Cleared ILS [Runway] Twenty-two left.

ENGINEER: Two thousand.

CAPTAIN: Select the ILS on my side.

CO-PILOT: The ILS in number one, one hundred ten point nine is set for two thousand feet.

ENGINEER: Localizer alive.

CAPTAIN: Give me flaps fourteen.

CO-PILOT: We are thirteen miles from the outer marker. Flaps fourteen.

CAPTAIN: Navigation number one. Did you already select flaps fourteen, no?

CO-PILOT: Yes, sir, [they] are set. Navigation number one.

NY APPROACH: Avianca zero five two heavy, speed one six zero, if practical.

CAPTAIN: Give me flaps twenty-five.

CO-PILOT: We have traffic ahead of us.

CAPTAIN: We can maintain one hundred and forty [mph] with this flap setting. How many miles is that thing located?

CO-PILOT: It is at seven miles, Commander, and we are at ten miles at the moment from the outer marker.

CAPTAIN: Reset frequency, the ILS please.

CO-PILOT: Now the course is going to be intercepted at the outer marker. This means there is not a problem, commander. Localizer to the left.

NY APPROACH: Avianca zero five two heavy, contact Kennedy Tower, one one niner point one, good day.

CO-PILOT: One one niner point one, so long. Kennedy Tower, Avianca zero five two established twenty-two left.

KENNEDY TOWER: Avianca zero five two heavy, Kennedy Tower, Twenty-two left. You're number three [to land] following [a Boeing] seven two seven traffic on, ah, niner mile final.

CO-PILOT: Avianca zero five two, roger.

CAPTAIN: Can I lower the landing gear yet?

CO-PILOT: No, I think it's too early now. If we lower the landing gear, we have to hold very high nose attitude.

ENGINEER: And it's not very . . .

KENNEDY TOWER: Avianca zero five two, what's your airspeed?

CO-PILOT: Avianca zero five two, one four zero knots.

CAPTAIN: They was asking for the American [Airlines 727 that was preceding the Avianca in for a landing].

KENNEDY TOWER: Avianca zero five two, can you increase your airspeed one zero knots?

CAPTAIN: One zero.

CO-PILOT: Okay, one zero knots, increasing.

KENNEDY TOWER: Increase, increase!

CAPTAIN: What?

CO-PILOT: Increasing.

CAPTAIN: What?

KENNEDY TOWER: Okay.

ENGINEER: Ten knots more.

CO-PILOT: Ten little knots more.

CAPTAIN: Here we go. Tell me things louder, because I'm not hearing it. [The Captain is hard of hearing]

CO-PILOT: We are three miles to the outer marker now.

CAPTAIN: Right resetting the ILS.

CO-PILOT: Here it is already intercepted. Glide slope alive.

CAPTAIN: I'm going to approach at one hundred and forty [mph]. It is what he wants, or what is the value he wants?

CO-PILOT: One hundred and fifty. We had one hundred and forty, and he required ten little knots more.

CAPTAIN: Lower the gear.

CO-PILOT: Gear down.

CAPTAIN: Mode selector approach land checklist.

They go through the landing checklist.

KENNEDY TOWER: Avianca zero five two, Twenty-two left, wind one niner zero at two zero. Cleared to land.

ENGINEER: [Landing] Gear.

CO-PILOT: Cleared to land, Avianca zero five two heavy. Wind check please?

KENNEDY TOWER: One niner zero at two zero.

CO-PILOT: Thank you. One hundred and ninety with twenty is in the wind.

CAPTAIN: With what?

KENNEDY TOWER: Avianca zero five two, say airspeed?

CO-PILOT: Zero five two is, ah, one four five knots.

KENNEDY TOWER TO ANOTHER FLIGHT: TWA eight oh one heavy, if feasible reduce airspeed one four five.

CAPTAIN: Give me fifty [flaps]. Are we cleared to land?

CO-PILOT: Yes, sir, we are cleared to land.

ENGINEER: Hydraulic pressure quantities, normal.

CO-PILOT: Stand by flaps fifty.

CAPTAIN: Give me fifty.

ENGINEER: All set for landing.

CO-PILOT: Below glide slope.

CAPTAIN: Confirm the wind.

KENNEDY TOWER: Avianca zero five two heavy, can you increase your airspeed one zero knots at all?

CO-PILOT: Yes, we're doing it.

KENNEDY TOWER: Okay, thank you.

CAPTAIN: Confirm the wind.

For the next minute and a half, the Avianca flight follows its glide path toward Kennedy International.

COCKPIT: [Ground proximity warning system sounds] *Whoop, Whoop, Pull up! Pull up!*

CO-PILOT: Sink rate. Five hundred feet.

CAPTAIN: Lights. Where is the runway? The runway! Where is it?

COCKPIT: [Ground proximity warning system sounds] *Glideslope.*

CO-PILOT: I don't see it! I don't see it!

CAPTAIN: Give me the landing gear up. Landing gear up.

COCKPIT: [Sound of landing gear warning horn]

CAPTAIN: Request another traffic pattern.

CO-PILOT TO KENNEDY TOWER: [We are] executing a missed approach, Avianca zero five two heavy.

ENGINEER: Smooth with the nose, smooth with the nose, smooth with the nose.

KENNEDY TOWER: Avianca zero five two heavy, roger. Ah, climb and maintain two thousand, turn left, heading one eight zero.

At this point, the Avianca flight, having missed its approach, goes around.

CAPTAIN TO COCKPIT CREW: We don't have the fuel [to go around] . . .

CO-PILOT: Maintain two thousand feet, one eight zero on the heading.

CAPTAIN: Flaps twenty five. I don't know what happened with the runway. I didn't see it.

ENGINEER: I didn't see it.

CO-PILOT: I didn't see it.

KENNEDY TOWER: Avianca zero five two, you are making a left turn, correct sir?

CAPTAIN: Tell them we are in emergency.

ENGINEER: Two thousand feet.

CO-PILOT TO KENNEDY TOWER: That's [turn] right to one eight zero on the heading, and, ah, we'll try [to land] once again. We're running out of fuel.

The Co-pilot mentions to the Tower that they are low on fuel, but he does not *declare an emergency; the declaration itself must be made in order for the declaring flight to be given emergency priorities to land.*

KENNEDY TOWER: Okay.
CAPTAIN: What did [Kennedy Tower] say?
CO-PILOT: Maintain two thousand feet, one eight on the heading. I already advise him that we are going to attempt again, because we now can't.
CAPTAIN: Advise [Kennedy Tower] we are [in an] emergency! Did you tell him?
CO-PILOT: Yes, sir. I already advised him.
CAPTAIN: Flaps four . . . fifteen.
KENNEDY TOWER: Avianca zero five two heavy, continue the left turn, heading one five zero, maintain two thousand.
CAPTAIN: They [told] us to reduce airspeed, that's the thing, man. Hundred and fifty [mph].
CO-PILOT: One hundred and fifty [mph] on the heading.
CAPTAIN: Flaps fifteen.

CO-PILOT TO NY APPROACH: Approach, Avianca zero five, ah, two heavy – we just missed [our] approach, and ah, we're maintaining two thousand and five on the . . .
NY APPROACH: Avianca zero five two heavy, New York, good evening. Climb and maintain three thousand.
CAPTAIN: Advise him we don't have fuel.

The Co-pilot still does not declare a fuel emergency.

CO-PILOT TO NY APPROACH: Climb and maintain three thousand, and ah, we're running out of fuel, sir.
NY APPROACH: Okay, fly heading zero eight zero.
CAPTAIN TO CO-PILOT: Did you already advise that we don't have fuel?
CO-PILOT: Yes sir, I already advised him . . . We are going to maintain three thousand feet, and he's going to get us back.
CAPTAIN: Okay.
NY APPROACH: Avianca zero five two heavy, turn left, heading zero seven zero.
CO-PILOT: Heading zero seven zero, Avianca zero five two heavy.
NY APPROACH: And Avianca zero five two

heavy, ah, I'm going to bring you about fifteen miles Northeast, and then turn you back onto the approach. Is that fine with you and your fuel?

CO-PILOT: I guess so, thank you very much.

CAPTAIN: What did he say?

ENGINEER: The guy [the controller] is angry.

CO-PILOT: Fifteen miles in order to get back to the localizer.

CAPTAIN: I'm going to follow this . . .

CO-PILOT: We must follow the identified ILS.

CAPTAIN: To die. Take it easy, take it easy.

CO-PILOT TO KENNEDY TOWER: Ah, can you give us a final now? Avianca zero five two heavy.

NY APPROACH: Avianca zero five two, affirmative, sir. Turn left, heading zero four zero.

ENGINEER: I have the [landing] lights on.

NY APPROACH TO ANOTHER FLIGHT: TWA eight zero one heavy, turn left, heading two five zero, you're one five miles from the outer marker. Maintain two thousand until established on the localizer. Cleared for ILS two two left.

CO-PILOT: Avianca zero five two heavy, left turn two five zero, and ah, we're cleared for ILS.

CAPTAIN: What heading? Tell me.

CO-PILOT: Two five zero.

NY APPROACH: Avianca fifty two, climb and maintain three thousand [feet].

COCKPIT: [Sound of landing gear warning horn]

CO-PILOT TO PILOT: Ah, negative, sir. We [are] just running out of fuel. We're okay three thousand. Now okay.

CAPTAIN: No, no, three . . . three thousand, three thousand.

NY APPROACH: Okay, turn left, heading three one zero, sir.

CO-PILOT: Three one zero, Avianca zero five two.

CAPTAIN: Tell me . . .

CO-PILOT: Three one zero in the . . .

CAPTAIN: Flaps fourteen.

CO-PILOT: Three one zero.

ENGINEER: No, sir, are in . . .

CAPTAIN: Set flaps fourteen.

NY APPROACH: Avianca fifty two, fly heading of three six zero, please.

CO-PILOT: Fourteen degrees.

CAPTAIN: Tell me heading. What?

CO-PILOT: Okay, we'll maintain three six zero now.

NY APPROACH: Okay, and you're number two [in line] for the approach. I just have to give you enough room so you can make it without, ah, having to [go around] again.

CO-PILOT: Okay, we're number two and flying three six zero now.

CAPTAIN: Three sixty, no?

CO-PILOT: Three sixty.

CAPTAIN: Flaps fourteen.

NY APPROACH TO TWA FLIGHT 801: TWA eight zero one heavy, you're eight miles behind a heavy jet [Avianca]. Contact Kennedy Tower, one one niner point one. Thanks for the help.

TWA 801 TO NY APPROACH: Okay, eight oh one roger and what's his ground . . . what's his airspeed, do you know?

NY APPROACH: Ah, he's indicating ten knots slower, eight miles.

TWA 801: Okay, thank you.

NY APPROACH TO PAN AM 1812: Clipper eighteen twelve heavy, speed one six zero, if practical.

PAN AM 1812: Eighteen twelve heavy slowing to one fifty.

NY APPROACH: Avianca zero five two heavy, turn left, heading three three zero.

CO-PILOT: Three three zero on the heading, Avianca zero five two. Three three zero, the heading.

ENGINEER: Flame out! Flame out on engine number four.

The tanks are out of fuel.

COCKPIT: [Sound of momentary power interruption to the CVR]

CAPTAIN: Flame out on it [the engine].

ENGINEER: Flame out on engine number three, essential on number two, one number one.

CAPTAIN: Show me the runway.

CO-PILOT TO NY APPROACH: Avianca zero five two, we just, ah, lost two engines and, ah, we need priority please.

NY APPROACH: Avianca zero five two, turn left, heading two five zero, intercept the localizer.

COCKPIT: [Sound of engine spooling down]

CO-PILOT: Two five zero. Roger.

CAPTAIN: Select the ILS.

NY APPROACH: Avianca zero five two heavy, you're one five miles [15 miles] from the outer marker, maintain two thousand [feet] until established on the localizer. Cleared for ILS Twenty-two left.

CO-PILOT: Roger, Avianca.

CAPTAIN: Did you select the ILS?

CO-PILOT: It is ready on two.

END OF TAPE

With its engines starved of fuel, the Avianca flight crashed into Cove Neck. The Captain, Co-pilot and Engineer died, as did five of the six Flight Attendants. Of the 158 souls on board, 73 perished; 82 were seriously injured; three people suffered minor injuries. The aircraft hit the ground at 9.35 p.m.

For seven minutes after take-off from Gregorio Luperon Airport, the Birgen Air Boeing 757, charter Flight ALW301, with 176 passengers and a crew of 13, flew into the late night darkness over the eastern Caribbean, en route to Frankfurt, Germany. During the take-off rollout, the pilot's airspeed indicator was inaccurate, and the co-pilot read out the speeds from the speedometer on his side of the cockpit. The crew saw no reason to abort the flight. However, the airspeed error, which was caused by a blocked pilot port outside of the aircraft (similar to the static ports on the doomed AeroPeru flight; see Chapter 2) confused the Pilot, who allowed the aircraft to stall. Without recovering, it fell into the sea five miles off the coast of the Dominican Republic and sank in 7,200 feet of water. The flight recorders were recovered in the deep on 28 February 1996 at a cost of $1.4 million.

We pick up the CVR transcript just as the Boeing 757 is accelerating down the airstrip for take-off.

TOWER: Have a nice flight.

COCKPIT: [Sound of increasing engine noise]

CO-PILOT: Power's set.

CAPTAIN: Okay, checked.

CO-PILOT: Eighty knots.

CAPTAIN: Checked. My airspeed indicator's not working.

CO-PILOT: Yes. Yours is not working. One twenty [mph].

CAPTAIN: Is yours working?

CO-PILOT: Yes, sir.

CAPTAIN: You tell me [the ground speed].

CO-PILOT: Vee one. Rotate.

CAPTAIN: Positive climb. Gear up.

CO-PILOT: Positive climb.

COCKPIT: [Sound of landing gear handle being moved]

CO-PILOT: Gear is up. LNAV [lateral navigation on autopilot]?

CAPTAIN: Yes, please.

CO-PILOT: LNAV.

CAPTAIN: Yes.

CO-PILOT: It began to operate.

CAPTAIN: Is it possible to turn off the [windshield] wipers?

CO-PILOT: Okay, wipers off.

COCKPIT: [Sound of windshield wipers stops]

CAPTAIN: Climb thrust.

CO-PILOT: Climb thrust.

CAPTAIN: VNAV [vertical navigation on the autopilot]

CO-PILOT: VNAV. Okay flap speed.

CAPTAIN: Flaps five, flaps one.

CO-PILOT: Flaps to one.

CAPTAIN: Gear handle off.

CO-PILOT: Gear handle's off.

CAPTAIN: Flaps up.

CO-PILOT: Flaps up.

CAPTAIN: [Begin] after take-off checklist.

CO-PILOT: After take-off checklist: landing gear up and off, flaps are up, checked up, altimeters later, after take-off completed.

CAPTAIN: Okay. Center autopilot on, please.

CO-PILOT: Center autopilot is on command.

CAPTAIN: Thank you. One zero one three. Rudder ratio, mach airspeed trim.

CO-PILOT: Yes, trim.

CAPTAIN: There is something wrong. There are some problems. Okay, there is something crazy. Do you see it?

CO-PILOT: There is something crazy there at this moment. Two hundred [mph] only is mine [speedometer] and [the speed is] decreasing, sir.

CAPTAIN: Both of [the speedometers] are wrong. What can we do? Let's check their circuit breakers.

CO-PILOT: Yes.

CAPTAIN: Alternate is correct.

CO-PILOT: The alternate one is correct.

CAPTAIN: As aircraft was not flying and [when it was] on ground, something happening . . . We don't believe [the speedometers].

Here we listen to the first signs of the Pilot's utter confusion.

ENGINEER: Shall I reset its circuit breaker?

CAPTAIN: Yes, reset it.

ENGINEER: To understand the reason?

CAPTAIN: Yeah.

COCKPIT: [Sound of aircraft overspeed warning]

CAPTAIN: Okay, it's no matter. Pull the airspeed [back]. We will see . . .

COCKPIT: [Overspeed warning stops]

CO-PILOT: Now it is three hundred and fifty [mph], yes.

CAPTAIN: Let's take that like this . . .

COCKPIT: [Sound of four warning alert

tones, sound of stick shaker starts indicating a stalling aircraft, and continues to end of recording, sound of four warning alert tones]

CO-PILOT: Sir . . . [put the] nose down.

ENGINEER: Now . . .

CO-PILOT: [Increase] thrust . . .

CAPTAIN: Disconnect the autopilot. Is autopilot disconnected?

CO-PILOT: Already disconnected, disconnected, sir.

CAPTAIN: [It will] not climb? What am I to do?

CO-PILOT: You may level off. Altitude okay. I am selecting the altitude hold, sir.

CAPTAIN: Select, select.

CO-PILOT: Altitude hold. Okay, five thousand feet.

CAPTAIN: Thrust levers, thrust thrust thrust thrust.

CO-PILOT: Retard.

CAPTAIN: Thrust. Don't pull back, don't pull back, don't pull back, don't pull back.

CO-PILOT: Okay open [the throttles], open . . .

CAPTAIN: Don't pull back. Please don't pull back.

CO-PILOT: Open, sir, open . . .

ENGINEER: Sir, pull up.

CAPTAIN: What's happening?

CO-PILOT: Oh, what's happening?

COCKPIT: [Ground Proximity Warning System Alarms *Whoop, Whoop, Pull up!* continues until the end of the recording]

CO-PILOT: Let's do like this . . .

END OF TAPE

The Birgen Air charter stalled and went into freefall for one minute and 41 seconds before hitting the sea. All souls aboard were lost.

A Boeing 707 configured as a radar E-3A for the US Air Force's 3rd Wing prepared for take-off at 7.47 on the morning of 22 September 1995, with a crew of four and 20 passengers. The morning was bright but overcast. Because of the fall season, flights of migrating Canadian geese had landed on the grasslands around the airfield, while other geese had taken off and were flying in the vicinity of the runway. The crew of the Air Force Boeing, which called itself Yukla 27-heavy, was aware of the birds.

We pick up the CVR just as Yukla 27 prepared for take-off.

TOWER: Yukla two seven heavy, the wind three one zero at one one, cleared for take-off [on] Runway Five. Traffic is a C-one-three-zero three miles north of Elmendorf northwest-bound, climbing out of two thousand.

COCKPIT: [Light switches]

CO-PILOT: [The C-one-three-zero] in sight. And Yukla two seven heavy cleared for take-off, traffic in sight. [To cockpit]: Cleared for take-off, crew.

FLIGHT ENGINEER: Check complete.

COCKPIT: [Engines spool up]

CAPTAIN: Engineer, set take-off power.

COCKPIT: [Engines spool up]

CAPTAIN: Eighty knots, co-pilot's aircraft [Co-pilot is flying the airplane]. Your airplane. Vee One. Rotate.

CO-PILOT: [Look at] all the birds.

FLIGHT ENGINEER: [There are a] lotta birds here.

At this point, the Nos. 1 and 2 engines ingested several geese, disintegrating the engine's fan blades.

CAPTAIN: Damn, we took one.

CO-PILOT: What do I got?

FLIGHT ENGINEER: We took two of 'em.

CAPTAIN: We got two motors.

ENGINEER: Flight start.

The Flight Engineer calls for an attempt to restart the failed engines.

CO-PILOT: Roger that.

CAPTAIN: Take me to override.

CO-PILOT: Go to override on, on the . . . Elmendorf Tower, Yukla two seven heavy has an emergency. Lost, ah, number two engine. We've taken some birds.

AN INSTRUCTOR FLIGHT ENGINEER IN COCKPIT: You're in override. There's the rudder.

FLIGHT ENGINEER: Got it.

INSTRUCTOR: You're in override.

CAPTAIN: Thank you.

ENGINEER: Starting [to] dump fuel.

CAPTAIN: Start dumping.

TOWER: Yukla two seven heavy, roger. Say intentions.

COCKPIT: [Stick shaker activates, continues until impact]

CO-PILOT: Yukla zero two heavy's coming back around for an emergency return. Lower the nose, lower the nose, lower the nose.

TOWER: Two seven heavy, roger.

CAPTAIN: Goin' down.

CO-PILOT: Oh my God.

CAPTAIN: Oh shit.

CO-PILOT: Okay, give it all you got, give it all you got. Two seven heavy, emergency . . .

TOWER: Roll the crash [equipment], roll the crash . . .

CO-PILOT ON PUBLIC ADDRESS SYSTEM: Crash [landing].

CAPTAIN: We're goin' in. We're goin' down.

END OF TAPE

The Air Force concluded that the cause of the crash was a 'multiple birdstrike' of Canadian geese in the No. 1 and No. 2 engines just after take-off. The aircraft crashed into woods and caught fire. All 24 souls aboard were lost.

El Al Flight 1862, with a crew of three and one passenger, was ferrying freight from Amsterdam's Schiphol Airport to Ben Gurion Airport in Israel. The Boeing 747 took off from Amsterdam Runway 01L at 5.21 in the afternoon. Six minutes later, at 5.27:30, as the aircraft was climbing through 6,500 feet, the No. 3 engine and the pylon that attaches the engine to the wing separated from the wing and slammed into the No. 4 engine, which also separated from the wing. The crew immediately declared an emergency and requested Runway 27 for landing. There is no identification on the CVR tape's transcript of the individual voices. 'Crew' is used instead of the individuals in the cockpit.

We pick up the CVR just as the crew is declaring an emergency.

CREW: El Al eighteen sixty-two, mayday, mayday, we have an emergency . . .

Air Traffic Control acknowledges the declaration of an emergency and immediately warns all other aircraft in the vicinity away from the airport with the term 'break'.

AIR TRAFFIC CONTROL: El Al eighteen sixty-two, roger. Break, KLM two three seven, turn left heading zero nine zero. El Al eighteen sixty-two, do you wish to return to Schiphol?
CREW: Affirmative. Mayday, mayday, mayday.
CONTROL: Turn right heading two six zero, field, eh . . . behind you, eh . . . in your – to the west, eh . . . distance eighteen miles.
CREW: Roger, we have fire on engine number three, we have fire on engine number three.
CONTROL: Roger, heading two seven zero for downwind.
CREW: Two seven zero downwind.
CONTROL: El Al eighteen sixty-two, surface wind forty at twenty-one knots.
CREW: Roger. El Al eighteen sixty-two, lost number three and number four engines, number three and number four engines.
CONTROL: Roger, eighteen sixty-two.

CREW: What will be the runway in use for me at Amsterdam?

CONTROL: Runway Six in use, sir. Surface wind forty at twenty-one knots . . .

CREW: We request [Runway] Twenty-seven for landing.

CONTROL: Roger, can you call Approach now, [tune to radio frequency] one twenty-one point two for your line-up?

CREW: One twenty-one point two, bye bye.

CONTROL: Bye.

CREW: Schiphol, El Al eighteen sixty-two, we have an emergency, eh . . . we're . . . number three and four engines inoperative . . . [returning] landing.

CONTROL: El Al eighteen sixty-two, roger, copied about your emergency, contact [radio frequency] one eighteen point four for your line-up.

CREW: One eighteen point four, bye. Schiphol, El Al eighteen sixty-two, we have an emergency, number three and number four engines inoperative, request [Runway] Twenty-seven for landing.

CONTROL: You request Twenty-seven, in that case heading three six zero . . . three six zero the heading. Descend to two thousand feet on one zero one two, mind, the wind is fifty at twenty-two.

CREW: Roger, can you say again the wind please?

CONTROL: Zero five zero at Twenty-two.

CREW: Roger, what heading for Runway Twenty-seven?

CONTROL: Heading three six zero, heading three six zero and [then] give you a right turn on, to cross the localizer first, and you've got only seven miles to go from [your] present position.

CREW: Roger, three six [heading three six zero] copied [understood].

CONTROL: El Al eighteen sixty-two, what is the distance you need to touchdown?

CREW: Twelve miles final we need for landing.

CONTROL: Yeah, how many miles [for] final [approach] . . . eh, correction . . . how many miles track miles you need?

CREW: We need . . . eh . . . a one two miles final for landing.

CONTROL: Okay, right right heading one zero zero, right right heading one hundred.

CREW: Heading one hundred.

CONTROL: El Al eighteen sixty-two, just to be sure, your engines number three and four are out?

CREW: Number three and four are out and

we have . . . eh . . . problems with our flaps.

CONTROL: Problem with the flaps, roger.

CREW: Heading one hundred, El Al eighteen sixty-two.

CONTROL: Thank you, eighteen sixty-two.

CREW: Okay, heading . . . eh . . . and turning, eh . . . maintaining . . .

CONTROL: Roger, eighteen sixty-two, your speed is?

CREW: Say again?

CONTROL: Your speed?

CREW: Our speed is . . . eh . . . two six zero.

CONTROL: Okay, you have around thirteen miles to go to touchdown. Speed is all yours. You are cleared to land Runway Twenty-seven.

CREW: Cleared to land Twenty-seven.

CONTROL: El Al eighteen sixty-two, a right right turn heading two seven zero. Adjust on the localizer. Cleared for approach.

CREW: Right, right two seven zero.

CONTROL: El Al eighteen sixty-two, you're about to cross the localizer due to your speed. Continue the right turn heading two nine zero, heading two nine zero, twelve track miles to go, twelve track miles to go.

CREW: Roger, two nine zero.

CONTROL: El Al eighteen sixty-two, further right, heading three one zero . . . heading three one zero.

CREW: Three one zero.

CONTROL: El Al eighteen sixty-two, continue descent one five hundred feet . . . one five hundred.

CREW: One five hundred, and we have a controlling problem.

CONTROL: You have a controlling problem as well, roger.

CREW: Going down eighteen sixty-two, going down . . . going down . . .

CONTROL: Copied, [you are] going down.

CREW: Raise all the flaps, all the flaps raise, lower the gear.

CONTROL: Yes, El Al eighteen sixty-two, your heading . . .

END OF TAPE

Metal fatigue was discovered in the inboard midspar of the No. 3 engine pylon. This caused the pylon and engine to separate from the wing. Part of the leading edge of the wing was damaged by the impact with the Nos. 3 and 4 engines, and, as a result, the use of several control systems was lost or limited. The investigator concluded that the flight crew had such limited control of the airplane that a safe landing was highly improbable, if not virtually impossible.

Flight 1862 crashed into an apartment building complex, killing the crew of three and the single passenger. 47 people on the ground died.

The Airbus of China Airlines Flight 140 took off from Taipei, Taiwan, for a flight to Nagoya, Japan, where it arrived over the outer marker at 8.12:26 p.m. The Co-pilot started an approach to Runway 34 ILS with auto-throttles engaged at an altitude of 1,070 feet when he inadvertently and unknowingly pushed the Take Off-Go Around [TOGA] switch on the control panel which automatically powered up the engines and configured the airplane for an aborted landing and 'go around' of the airport. Unaware of the instructions they had given to the autopilot, the crew fought the airplane to make it land. To remain on the glideslope, the co-pilot disengaged the auto-throttle, reduced thrust manually, and switched off the autopilot.

At 1,030 feet the crew commanded the autopilot to put them on the glideslope. But the autopilot reverted to the Go Around mode. To get back on the glideslope, the crew lowered the aircraft while the autopilot was telling the airplane to pitch up and go around. The Captain and Co-pilot were fighting the autopilots for control of the aircraft.

42 seconds after the mistaken Go Around selection, the crew disengaged the autopilots again, but the aircraft kept climbing. Eight seconds afterwards, the computer, which had been told to Go Around, triggered maximum thrust of the Airbus engines. The Captain pulled back on the engine thrust and the speed dropped. The Airbus stalled at 1,800 feet. The aircraft hit the ground tail-first 300 feet to the right of the runway and burst into flames.

The weather that evening was clear with light winds and nine miles of visibility.

The airbus was carrying a crew of 15 and 271 passengers.

We pick up the CVR tape with Flight 140 cleared for landing and on the glideslope. The Co-pilot is at the controls.

CAPTAIN: Engage it. Push it. It's too high. You . . . on Go Around mode. Don't worry, slowly, slowly, begin it. Support it firmly with your hand. Push, push it.
CO-PILOT: It could not be pushed.
CAPTAIN: Don't worry, do it slowly. Okay, I try.

CO-PILOT: I engage it. I engage it.

CAPTAIN: What is this?

CO-PILOT: I engage it.

CAPTAIN: Goddamn it! Why it comes in this way?

Flight 140 had aborted its landing approach, and the automatic Go Around system was pitching up the nose.

TOWER: Standby further instruction.

CREW: Aircraft will stall at this rate.

CO-PILOT: No way! No way!

CAPTAIN: Set, set, set it. Don't worry. Don't worry. Don't upset. Don't upset.

CABIN: [A recorded warning voice says, *Terrain Terrain*]

CREW: Power!

CABIN: [Stall warning says, *Pull up! Pull up!*]

CO-PILOT: Ah . . . no way! No way!

END OF TAPE.

The crew was confused about the autopilot and auto-throttle. The crew might have saved the aircraft even in the final seconds before it crashed if it had reverted to 'basic flight procedures' – indeed, if they had switched off the autopilot and flown the airplane with their own hands.

The crew of 15 died in the resulting, fiery crash; of the 271 souls aboard, all but seven perished.

Korean Airlines Flight 2033, an Airbus A300, was approaching a rain-slicked airport that summer morning, when a conflict arose between the Captain of the airplane and his Co-pilot.

The Co-pilot, Chung Chan Kuy, a Korean, asked Captain Barry Woods, a Canadian, several times whether he wanted to 'go around'. Apparently, the Co-pilot was concerned about the length of Runway 6. When the Captain told his Co-pilot not to 'go around', the Co-pilot grabbed for the throttles. Woods told him to 'Get off'.

They were flying through a tropical storm with winds that were gusting up to 30 mph.

We pick up the CVR tape just as the runway comes into sight.

CO-PILOT: Runway in sight, runway in sight.
CAPTAIN: I got it, I got it.
CO-PILOT: Okay. Right side? Right?
CAPTAIN: Yeah . . . Okay. Give me the, uh, four hundred [feet] . . . three . . . Minimum sink rate.

CO-PILOT: Sink rate, sink rate.
CAPTAIN: Okay, okay.
CO-PILOT: One hundred [feet]. Speed?
CAPTAIN: Yeah, fifty [feet].

At this juncture, the Co-pilot decides that there is insufficient distance for the Airbus to land safely without crossing the end of the runway. The Co-pilot, when the aircraft is only 30 feet off the ground, decides to 'go around' and pulls back on the yoke.

CO-PILOT: Go around, forty [feet], thirty [feet] . . .
CAPTAIN: Get your hands . . . Get off! Get off! Tell me what [the altitude] is. Twenty [feet]. Get off.
CO-PILOT: Go around?
CAPTAIN: No, no, ten, five [feet].

Here they touched down and the brakes and the thrust reversers were deployed; no matter. The Co-pilot still wanted to abort the landing and go around against the wishes of the Captain who was telling him not to go around but to brake the aircraft.

CAPTAIN: Reverse [engines]. Brake. What are you doing? Don't. What man . . . You're gonna kill us. Hold yoke.

COCKPIT: [Sound of crash]

The aircraft crashed through a fence and slid into a rice paddy on the side of the field, coming to a stop.

CAPTAIN: Yup, okay. You all right?

CO-PILOT: All right.

CAPTAIN: Okay. Get this off. What did you pull us off [for]? What did you pull us off [for]?

CO-PILOT: [I wanted to] go around . . . go around.

CAPTAIN: Yeah, but we were on . . . we were on the runway. Why did you pull us off? Okay, okay. We got to get out of here. Open your window.

COCKPIT: [Sound of opening the cockpit window]

CAPTAIN: Get your [evacuation] slide. Why did you pull us off? We had full reverse on. Pull the fire handles. Pull 'em.

CO-PILOT: Fire pulls.

CAPTAIN: Okay, get out. Get out.

END OF TAPE.

Miraculously, in spite of the airplane catching fire, the six-member cabin crew got all of the 152 passengers off the airplane safely, with only a few minor injuries. The Pilot and Co-pilot exited through the cockpit windows. The Airbus was a total write-off. Korean authorities contemplated bringing criminal charges against the Captain and Co-pilot of the aircraft.

JAL Flight 123, a Boeing 747, took off from Tokyo-Haneda at 6.12 p.m. for a flight to Osaka with 509 passengers and 15 crew members. At 6.24 p.m., while climbing through 23,900 feet at a speed of 345 mph, an unusual vibration and the sound of an impact signalled a catastrophic rupture of the aft bulkhead.

In the two minutes that followed the rupture, hydraulic pressure dropped. Ailerons, elevators and yaw damper – surfaces that control the direction and altitude of the aircraft – failed to work, and the altitude and speed changed in twenty-to-a-hundred-second cycles. The plane was out of control as it fell to 6,600 feet. The crew tried to use engine thrust to manoeuvre the aircraft. At 6,600 feet, the airspeed dropped dangerously to 124 mph. Then the aircraft climbed sharply to 13,400 feet and started to fall again. The aircraft finally brushed against a tree-covered ridge along a mountain but continued to fly for another three seconds until it struck another, nearby ridge and burst into flames.

It was the worst disaster in Japanese aviation history.

We begin the CVR tape just after the collapse of the aft bulkhead.

PUBLIC ADDRESS SYSTEM: Put on oxygen mask. Fasten seat belt. We are making an emergency descent.

FLIGHT ATTENDANT TO THE PASSENGERS ON PA SYSTEM: May we ask you passengers with infants . . . nearby passengers . . . please be ready.

CAPTAIN: Right turn. Right turn.

CO-PILOT: I did it.

CAPTAIN: Yes. Do not bank so steeply.

CO-PILOT: Yes, sir.

CAPTAIN: Do not bank so steeply.

CO-PILOT: Yes, sir.

CAPTAIN: Recover it.

CO-PILOT: It does not recover.

CAPTAIN: Pull up.

13 seconds go by while the crew tries to gain control of the aircraft.

CAPTAIN: All hydraulics failed.
CO-PILOT: Yes, sir.
CAPTAIN: Descend.
CO-PILOT: Yes, sir.

Another 15 seconds go by.

CAPTAIN: Hydro [hydraulic] pressure is lost.
CO-PILOT: All lost?
CAPTAIN: All lost.

Two and a half minutes go by.

ENGINEER: How about cabin pressure? Have cabin masks dropped? So? Well, cabin pressure, please.

Slightly more than a minute passes.

ENGINEER: Cabin pressure dropped. What? More aft . . . ah. What was damaged? Where? Coat room? Ah, coat room . . . general . . . It dropped in baggage space. It would be better to land. All persons inhale [into] masks. Captain?
CAPTAIN: Yes?
ENGINEER: Do we put on [our] masks?

CAPTAIN: Yes, it would be better.
ENGINEER: I think it would be better to inhale emergency mask.
CAPTAIN: Yes.

For another three minutes, the Boeing 747 flounders with the Pilot using the engines to 'fly' the airplane by applying power to one side or the other in order to steer the aircraft left for right.

CAPTAIN: Nose down. Lower nose.
CO-PILOT: Yes, sir.
CAPTAIN: Lower nose.
CO-PILOT: Yes, sir.
CAPTAIN: Lower nose.
CO-PILOT: Yes, sir.
CAPTAIN: Stop saying that. Do it with both hands, with both hands.
CO-PILOT: Yes, sir.
ENGINEER: Do we [put the landing] gear down?
CO-PILOT: Gear down?
CAPTAIN: Speed does not drop.
CO-PILOT: Speed does not drop.
CAPTAIN: Lower nose.
CO-PILOT: Yes, sir.

For the next ten minutes, the crew wrestles with the controls and the throttles, from applying power to lowering the nose.

CAPTAIN: Power, power, lower nose. It is heavy. Lower nose slightly more. It is heavy. It is heavy. Oh, it is heavy.

CO-PILOT: What about flap? Do I extend it?

CAPTAIN: It is a bit too early.

CO-PILOT: It is too early?

CAPTAIN: It is too early, too early. Was gear extended [lowered]?

CO-PILOT: Gear was extended.

CAPTAIN: Lower nose.

FLIGHT ATTENDANT TO PASSENGERS ON PA SYSTEM: Those passengers who accompany babies, please keep your heads on seat backs and hold your babies firmly. Did you fasten seat belts? All tables are retracted. Please check it . . . Sometimes we land without notice . . . We keep contact with ground . . .

CAPTAIN: Lower nose. It may be hopeless. It is a mountain? Raise nose.

CO-PILOT: Yes, sir.

CAPTAIN: Control to right. Right turn. Raise nose. We may hit the mountain.

CO-PILOT: Yes, sir.

CAPTAIN: Right turn.

COCKPIT: [Warning sounds of Ground Proximity Warning System]

CAPTAIN: Max power.

CO-PILOT: Max power.

CAPTAIN: Hold out. Left turn.

CO-PILOT: Yes, sir.

ENGINEER: Hold out.

CAPTAIN: Left turn, now . . . Left turn.

CO-PILOT: Decrease power slightly.

CAPTAIN: Right, right . . . Lower nose.

CO-PILOT: Fully controlled now.

COCKPIT: [Warning sounds stop]

CO-PILOT: It is totally ineffective . . .

CAPTAIN: Lower nose.

CO-PILOT: Good.

CAPTAIN: Here we go.

CO-PILOT: Yes, sir.

ENGINEER: Do I increase power?

CAPTAIN: Power, power.

COCKPIT: [Warning sounds]

CAPTAIN: Power. Let's increase power, power . . .

COCKPIT: [Stall warning sounds] *Pull up! Pull up!*

CAPTAIN: Ah, it is hopeless. Max power.

CO-PILOT OR ENGINEER: Max power.

CAPTAIN: Stall. Let's hang tough. Hold out.

CO-PILOT: Yes, sir.

CAPTAIN: Lower nose. Hold out, hold out.

CO-PILOT: Fully controlled.

ENGINEER: Speed is controlled by power. How about power control? Power control, Captain?

CAPTAIN: Yes. Speed is two twenty knots.

ENGINEER: Yes, sir.

CAPTAIN: Do not lower nose. It increases speed.

CO-PILOT: Yes, sir.

CAPTAIN: It's going down.

CO-PILOT: Yes, sir. Raise nose, raise.

Five minutes go by, while the crew struggles with the controls.

CAPTAIN: Raise nose, raise nose, raise nose. Stop flap. Do not extend flap so deeply. Flap up, flap up, flap up, flap up, flap up.

CO-PILOT: Yes, sir.

CAPTAIN: Power, power. Flap.

CO-PILOT: I am retracting [the flaps].

CAPTAIN: Raise nose, raise nose, power.

COCKPIT: [Ground Proximity warning] *Sink rate. Pull up! Pull up! Pull up! Pull up! Pull up!*

COCKPIT: [Sound of collision with the first peak]

Three seconds go by.

COCKPIT: [Sound of collision with the second peak]

Two seconds go by.

END OF TAPE.

Metal fatigue cracks caused the aft bulkhead to collapse, which broke through the hydraulic controls that extend along the fuselage to the cockpit of the Boeing 747. 520 souls died that day. Four passengers miraculously survived. Although none of the information appeared on the CVR tape, the passengers were aware of their peril. After the crash several last letters were discovered in the wreckage from passengers to loved ones, saying goodbye.

The cockpit crew was about to show off the new Air France Airbus A320 that spring day to crowds waiting below at the Habsheim Airport. Demonstrating the new airplane's capabilities to those on the ground and to 130 passengers, mostly members of the press, who were riding along, the crew planned two passes of the airfield, one a low-level, high-speed 'fly by'. For everyone that day, it would be a demonstration from hell.

The crew started out in a jovial mood, laughing at the antiquity of an airplane that had landed and crossed their path as they taxied the Airbus out for take-off. A Flight Attendant chatted as the crew went through its preflight checklist.

We pick up the CVR as the Co-pilot asks the Captain to explain what they are going to do for the demonstration.

CAPTAIN: Okay, then. [We're going to] Take-off, [then make a] right turn. Leave the flap at one. Anyway, we do normal take-off, retract the landing gear and with flaps at one, we go nice and easy. As soon as we have formally identified it [the airport], we extend the flaps to three, landing gear extended, [and we] do the flyover at one hundred feet, landing gear out, and then you leave it to me . . .

CAPTAIN TO CO-PILOT: I've done it twenty times, that one.

CO-PILOT: Okay, we're agreed.

CAPTAIN TO CO-PILOT: And then, after, we bring everything [flaps] in, move off and give it all it's got to three four zero knots [391 mph], and [on the] second [flyover], you also go over at one hundred feet. And there's no need to pull two point five gs, as back there [in the passenger cabin], they won't like it.

CO-PILOT: Okay, all that.

TOWER: ACF two ninety-six Q Basle?

CO-PILOT: Go ahead.

TOWER: Yes, two ninety-six Q, can you tell me what altitude you want?

CO-PILOT TO TOWER: Two thousand [feet].

CAPTAIN: Roger, one thousand feet to get there, one thousand feet to get there, one thousand feet go around . . .

CO-PILOT: Yes, after take-off, we'll take a right turn one thousand feet to the flying club, then there we'll make two flyovers, the second [one] at high speed, and then we'll negotiate clearance with you to go to . . . hmmmm.

CAPTAIN: Hericourt.

TOWER: Roger, two ninety-six Q.

CAPTAIN: So it's one thousand feet Fox Echo.

CO-PILOT TO TOWER: Well, it would be good if we could have clearance before the second flyover as we'll be passing at high speed, like that. We could climb quickly.

TOWER: Roger, two ninety-six Q. You confirm one thousand feet above ground then?

CO-PILOT: One thousand feet above ground, and by right turn there. Then we'll descend for low altitude flyover of the airfield there.

TOWER: Okay, I'll call you.

Still on the taxiway, the crew goes over the plans for the flyover several times. They inform the tower of what they are planning, and they ask for clearances. However, the Co-pilot still isn't clear about what he is supposed to do.

CO-PILOT: Between the two [flyovers], when I take it for the high-speed flyover, you negotiate the one ninety degree clearance so that we can get out of there and do a pull-out at two gs.

CAPTAIN: No, don't pull out at two point five gs, as yesterday we did two gs. Two point five gs in training, and I've had enough of that, I have . . .

PURSER COMES INTO COCKPIT: In short, what are we doing?

CAPTAIN: We take off, fly to the Habsheim airfield. There we do a low-altitude flyover, bank, accelerate, fly over at top speed and get out of there.

CO-PILOT TO PURSER: Yes? You were saying?

PURSER: No, but I was saying [that] the cabin is ready.

CO-PILOT: You stay seated during the complete flyover.

PURSER: About the announcements. You're doing something?

CAPTAIN: I'm going to tell them [the passengers], yes. The announcements, I'll do them.

PURSER: Okay. There are also some [Germans on board].

CAPTAIN TO PASSENGERS OVER PA SYSTEM:

Ladies and gentlemen, hello and welcome aboard this Airbus Three twenty, number three of the series for Air France and which has only been in service for two days. We shall take off for a short tourist flight starting at the Habsheim flying club where we will do two flyovers to demonstrate the [quality] of French aviation . . .
TOWER: Hello, ACF two ninety-six Q. Hold before Runway Sixteen.

For the next two minutes, the crew goes through the pre-take-off checklist. The two men discuss the computer flight-control imputs. The Flight Attendant comes in to the cockpit.

CAPTAIN TO FLIGHT ATTENDANT: What? No. I'll tell you something. You're not used to cockpits, are you? But like this, when we're really busy, as you can see, you should not speak, ah, shouldn't bother to speak, shouldn't bother the pilots. Eh? You see how it is?

The Captain and the Co-pilot converse with two passengers who come up to the cockpit. They discuss the possibility of flying over another destination, Meribel, for which they do not have clearance, after the flyover of Habsheim.

TOWER: Two ninety-six Q, clear for take-off Runway Sixteen, wind calm.
CAPTAIN: Take-off. Go.
COCKPIT: [Sound of engine acceleration]
CO-PILOT: Parameters normal.
CAPTAIN: Gut [Good]. One hundred [mph].

The Co-pilot seems amazed at the flight characteristics of the new aircraft.

CO-PILOT: It's [the computer] is requesting 'climb', the bastard. You see that?
CAPTAIN: Yeah, that happens.
CO-PILOT: Yeah, yeah. Vee One, Vee Rotate . . .
CAPTAIN: Positive climb. Gear up.
CO-PILOT: Gear up.
CAPTAIN: Gear up?
COCKPIT: [Reduction in engine noise]
CO-PILOT: Gear up, flaps one, after take-off check list is completed, except for flaps.
CAPTAIN: I'm disengaging the auto-throttle.
COCKPIT: [Repetitive gongs]
CAPTAIN: That's the landing gear, that. It's not important. Kill it, eh [the gong]? Oh, kill it. It gets on my nerves, that one.

CO-PILOT: You're eight nautical miles there. You'll soon see it [Habsheim Airfield]. There's the motorway.

CAPTAIN: We'll leave the motorway to the left, won't we . . . It's to the left . . . No, to the right of the motorway.

CO-PILOT: It's slightly to the right of the motorway. So you, you leave the motorway on the left.

CAPTAIN: Okay. As soon as we identify [Habsheim airfield], we [will] descend very quickly then . . .

CO-PILOT: Leave everybody fastened in [their seat belts].

TOWER: Roger, ACF two-ninety-six. You can contact Habsheim one twenty-five point two five. Goodbye.

CO-PILOT TO TOWER: One twenty-five point two five, good bye. Habzeim? [To the Captain] That's it, no?

CAPTAIN [Corrects his pronunciation]: Habsheim. Habs . . . Heim . . .

CO-PILOT: Habsheim. Habsheim Air Charter, two ninety-six Q. Hello.

CAPTAIN: There's the airfield. It's there. You got it, have you?

TOWER: Two ninety-six Q, hello.

CAPTAIN: What? We're coming into view of the airfield for flyover.

TOWER: Yes, I can see you. You're cleared, eh. Sky is clear.

CAPTAIN: Gear down.

CO-PILOT TO TOWER: Okay, we're going in for the low altitude, low speed flyover, two ninety-six Q.

TOWER: Roger.

CAPTAIN: Flaps two.

CO-PILOT: Good. Gear is down. Flaps two.

CAPTAIN: Flaps three.

CO-PILOT: Flaps three.

CAPTAIN: That's the airfield. You confirm?

CO-PILOT: Affirmative.

COCKPIT: [Gongs sound to warn of 'Too Low Terrain', 'Two Hundred' [feet]]

CO-PILOT: Okay, you're at a hundred feet. Watch, watch . . .

COCKPIT: [Mechanical voice says, *One hundred* then *Fifty* and *Forty* and *Thirty*, as it calls out the altitude in feet]

CAPTAIN: Okay, I'm okay there. Disconnect auto-throttle.

CO-PILOT: Watch out for the pylons ahead. See 'em?

CAPTAIN: Yeah, yeah. Don't worry.

CO-PILOT: Go around track.

COCKPIT: [Increase in engine speed; noises of impact]

CAPTAIN: Shit.

END OF TAPE.

The crew fought the autopilot and finally lost control of the Airbus, which could not regain enough altitude to clear the trees at the end of the Habsheim airfield. Three passengers died in the resulting crash. A combination of errors, including Pilot errors and confusion over the operation of the Airbus's computer command control, caused the crash. The tragedy was a dreadful embarrassment to French aviation.

Delta Air Lines' Lockheed L-1011 TriStar, Flight 191, was on final approach into Dallas–Fort Worth from Fort Lauderdale-Hollywood, Florida, when it encountered heavy thunderstorms. While approaching Runway 17L, the crew could see flashes of lightning in a cumulonimbus cloud. The TriStar, with a crew of eleven and 152 passengers, stayed on the approach despite the rain and wind. At 6,300 feet from the end of the runway, the TriStar entered a low-level microburst, which created massive wind shear. At that time, the crew lacked definitive, real-time training to learn to avoid and escape low-level wind shear. Caught by surprise, the crew could only sit by helplessly. As with other crashes, the double tragedy of Delta 191 was the ignorance of the crew. They simply did not understand the nature of wind shear.

We start the CVR at the moment when the tower asks another Delta Jet Flight 963 – to change direction. That crew demurs, because it sights the thunderstorms ahead. The cockpit crew of Delta 191 hears the exchange.

TOWER: Delta nine six three, I got an area twelve miles wide [that] all the aircraft are going through. All the aircraft are going through there. [It's a] good ride. I'll have [you] turn back in before you get to the weather [thunderstorms].

Now, the Captain and Co-pilot of Delta 191 can be heard on the cockpit tape.

CO-PILOT: It would be nice if we could deviate to the south of two five zero.
CAPTAIN: Somebody [Delta Flight 963] just ahead of us tried and they wouldn't let them do it. They're working a twelve-mile corridor. The airplanes that have been going through there have been all right.
TOWER: Delta one ninety-one, descend and maintain one zero thousand [10,000 feet], altimeter two niner niner one.
ENGINEER: Think that might have been for us, guys.
CAPTAIN TO TOWER: Sorry, was that for Delta one ninety-one?
TOWER: One ninety-one, descend and maintain one zero thousand [10,000 feet],

the altimeter two niner niner one, and suggest now a heading of two five zero . . . We have a good area there to go through.

CAPTAIN TO TOWER: Well, I'm looking at a [microburst] cell at about heading, ah, two five five, and it's a pretty good-size cell, and I'd rather not go through it. I'd rather go around it, one way or another.

TOWER: I can't take you south. I gotta line of departures to the south. I've had about sixty aircraft go through this area out here, ten . . . twelve miles wide. They're getting a good ride. No problems.

CAPTAIN: Well, I see a cell now about heading two four zero.

TOWER: Okay . . . When I can, I'll turn you. It'll be about the zero one zero radial.

CO-PILOT TO CAPTAIN: He [the Tower] must be going to turn us before we get to that area [of thunderstorms and cells].

CAPTAIN: Put the girls down [tell the Flight Attendants to be seated].

COCKPIT: [Sound of chime]

About three minutes later, the crew questions the experience of the Controller in the Tower.

CAPTAIN: Getting kind of hot in the oven with this Controller. See? That's what the lack of experience does. You're in good shape. I'm glad we didn't have to go through that mess. I thought sure [the controller] was going to send us through it.

ENGINEER: Looks like it's raining over Fort Worth.

CO-PILOT: Yeah.

Five minutes go by. The crew begins its final approach check.

TOWER: Attention, all aircraft listening . . . There's a little rain shower just north of the airport and they're starting to make ILS approaches . . .

Delta 191 descends through 7,000 to 5,000 feet. After completing more pre-landing checks, the Pilot sees the storm out of the window.

TOWER: Delta one ninety-one, turn left heading one nine zero, and I'll turn you right back on [down wind] in just a second.

CREW [unidentified]: All that screwing around for nothing.

CO-PILOT: We're going to get our airplane washed [with rain].

CAPTAIN: What?

CO-PILOT: We're going to get our airplane washed.

For the next three minutes, Delta 191 lines up for approach and landing.

TOWER: And we're getting some variable winds out there due to a shower on short out there, north end of DFW [Dallas–Fort Worth].

CREW [unidentified, either Captain or Co-pilot]: Stuff [thunderstorm] is moving in.

CAPTAIN: One six zero is the speed.

CAPTAIN: Tower, Delta one ninety-one, out here in the rain. Feels good.

ENGINEER: Landing gear [down].

TOWER: Delta one ninety-one heavy, one seven left, cleared to land, winds zero nine zero at five gusting to one five.

CO-PILOT: All right. Landing gear?

CAPTAIN: Down, three green [confirmation that gear is down].

ENGINEER: Flaps, slats.

CO-PILOT: Straight through eighteen [hundred feet].

COCKPIT: [Sound of altitude horn]

CO-PILOT: There's lightning coming out of that one [cloud].

CAPTAIN: What?

CO-PILOT: There's lightning coming out of that [cloud].

CAPTAIN: Where?

CO-PILOT: Right ahead of us. We're too late.

TOWER TO A DELTA FLIGHT ON THE TAXIWAY: Delta ten sixty-one, cross one seven right without delay, ground point six five after you cross.

DELTA 1061: Say again, ten sixty-one.

TOWER: Ten sixty-one, cross one seven right, ground point six five.

CAPTAIN: How about the DME [Distance Measuring Equipment]?

CO-PILOT: Well, you haven't had it for the last five minutes.

TOWER TO OTHER TAXIING AIRPLANES: Delta nine sixty-three and American six-nineteen, cross one seven right, ground point six-five, after you cross.

Up to this point in the flight, neither the passengers nor the crew had a hint of what was to come; as far as the passengers were concerned, their flight was nearly over. The crew was probably feeling some anxiety about the weather, but because other flights had landed safely only minutes in front of them, they did not appear to be overly concerned.

FLIGHT ENGINEER: A thousand [feet].
CO-PILOT: One thousand feet.
CAPTAIN: Watch your speed.
TOWER TO A TAXIING AIRCRAFT: American One six six contact departure.

Now, the Delta TriStar enters the microburst and the wind shear.

CAPTAIN: You're gonna lose it all of the sudden. There it is. Push it up, push it way up!
CO-PILOT: [Pull] Way up.
CAPTAIN: Way up. Way up.
COCKPIT: [Sound of engine high rpm]
CAPTAIN: That's it. Hang on to the son of a bitch.

CO-PILOT: What's the vee-ref?
TOWER TO A TAXIING AIRCRAFT: American five eighty-six, taxi into position and hold one seven right.
TAXIING AIRCRAFT AA586: Position and hold.
COCKPIT: [Ground Proximity Warning, mechanical] *Whoop, Whoop, Pull Up!*
CAPTAIN: Toga! [Go around, abort landing approach]
COCKPIT: [*Whoop, Whoop, Pull Up!* Sound of Go Around initiation, beeps]
CAPTAIN: Push it way up!

Delta 191 hit the ground 6,300 feet short of the runway. It then slid along the ground and struck a car on a highway, collided with two water tanks, broke up and burst into flames. Eight of the 11 crew died. 26 of the 152 passengers survived the crash.

The events surrounding the crash of Southern Air Transport's Flight 15 unfolded a little like a mystery.

The Lockheed L-382G four-propeller cargo aircraft arrived in Texas in the early morning hours, with a crew of three and a cargo of Class B and Class C-3 explosives (dynamite propellants and rocket motors for fighter jet ejection seats). Southern Air was a domestic airline that hauled cargo for the military. Flight 15, known as Logair 15, had originated at Hill Air Force Base, Utah. The new crew had arrived early in the morning of 4 October at Kelly Air Force Base Flight Operations, where they spoke briefly with the retiring crew, just in from Utah. The retiring captain said the Lockheed was 'in good shape'.

Flight 15's Flight Engineer supervised the loading and unloading of cargo to make certain that each of the ten pallets of cargo was secured both forward and aft on the airplane's floor locks. The military loading supervisor recalled later that the airplane's elevator – the control surface on the tail that flies the airplane up or down – was raised to prevent its being damaged during the loading operations.

By four that morning, the crew of Flight 15 was ready to leave. It went through all the pre-start flight checks before taxiing out to Runway 15. At 4.05 a.m., the Captain notified the tower that they were waiting for permission to take-off, on a Visual Flight Rules ascent.

We pick up the CVR tape here.

TOWER: Logair One-five, one thousand feet closed wind one-five-zero at four – cleared for take-off.

CO-PILOT: One-five, roger. Transponders on.

CAPTAIN: Okay, before-take-off check . . .

ENGINEER: Okay, whenever you're ready for [engines] one and four, Captain.

CAPTAIN: One and four normal.

CO-PILOT: Off at zero five [4.05 a.m.]

CAPTAIN: Yeah.

CO-PILOT: Final.

ENGINEER: Before-take-off check is complete.

CO-PILOT: Finals clear.

CAPTAIN: Okay eight, twelve, twenty.

ENGINEER: Lights out.

CAPTAIN: Set max power. Airspeed's alive.

CO-PILOT: Sixty knots.

CAPTAIN: My yoke [my control of take-off].

CO-PILOT: Your yoke. Vee one. Rotate [leave ground].

Two seconds go by, after leaving ground at rotation.

CAPTAIN: Jesus Christ, help me on my yoke. Help me on the yoke. God. Help. Push forward.

CO-PILOT: I can't get it down.

At this point the aircraft was about 700 feet off the ground. Witnesses reported seeing an abnormally steep climb. Then the airplane abruptly banked left. It continued to roll to the left.

CAPTAIN: You got this damn thing in here.

ENGINEER: Come on, pull it . . . Pull it back a little. Pull it back a little. Did you pull it back?

CAPTAIN: Okay, let me roll it into a bank.

CO-PILOT: What's the airspeed doing?

CAPTAIN: Damn it. Okay, come on. Get it over.

CO-PILOT: We're dead.

CAPTAIN: Lots of rudder, lots of rudder.

ENGINEER: Okay, it's clear now.

COCKPIT: [Sound of Ground Proximity Warning Horn, and recorded voice] *Whoop, Whoop, Pull up! Pull up!*]

ENGINEER: Oh, God.

END OF TAPE

Flight 15 rolled and went straight into the ground between two hangers. The airplane exploded on impact, causing a severe fire.

What had caused the disaster later seemed particularly tragic in light of the care and professionalism of the crew. A metal device called a gust lock – a t-shaped piece of aluminium four inches long and ten inches wide – was jammed in the Co-pilot's control yoke. The retiring crew of Flight 15 had inserted the lock behind the control yoke on the Co-pilot's side of the cockpit in order to raise the elevator control surface on the horizontal stabilizer in the tail of the airplane during the cargo loading operation. The gust lock was meant to be removed before take-off, but the incoming Co-pilot had failed to notice it. The Captain, who was flying the take-off, did not feel the jammed elevator until he had rotated the aircraft. By then those aboard were all but doomed. All three died. The hull-loss value was $8 million.

That day, just after noon, Atlantic Southeast Airlines' Flight 529, a turbo-prop commuter flight, took off from Atlanta Hartsfield International Airport bound for Gulfport, Mississippi, with 26 passengers and a crew of three. The twin-engined Embraer EMB-120RT airplane, manufactured in Brazil, had flown for 17,151 hours in 18,171 take-off-landing cycles.

At the time of departure, the clouds were at 200 feet scattered with a ceiling of 1,600 feet broken, 3,400 feet overcast. Visibility was two miles. There was light rain and fog; temperature was 73°F; winds were light. The aircraft was carrying 350 gallons of fuel equally distributed in the left and right side wing tanks.

We pick up the CVR nine minutes after Flight 529 took off from Atlanta, climbing to 12,000 feet.

CAPTAIN: Tell Robin [the lone Flight Attendant in the back of the aircraft] it'll just be a couple of minutes [before the ride will] smooth out.

STEWARDESS COMING TO COCKPIT: Hello.

CO-PILOT: Hey, Robin.

FLIGHT ATTENDANT: Hi.

CO-PILOT: It'll be just a couple more minutes like this; it'll smooth out.

FLIGHT ATTENDANT: Uh, a couple more minutes and then I can get up?

CO-PILOT: Yes, ma'am.

FLIGHT ATTENDANT: All right, thank you.

CO-PILOT: See ya.

ATLANTA CONTROL: AC five twenty-nine, climb and maintain one three thousand [13,000 feet].

CAPTAIN: Thirteen. Props ninety.

CO-PILOT ON PA SYSTEM: Ladies and gentlemen, good afternoon. Welcome aboard Atlantic Southeast Airlines Flight Five twenty-nine, service to Gulfport. We're passing through thirteen thousand feet. Captain has turned off the fasten-seat-belt sign. You are free to move about the cabin as you wish . . . Gulfport on the hour is calling for partly cloudy skies, temperature of eighty degrees, and winds ten miles an hour out of the north-east. [If] there's anything we can do to make your flight more enjoyable, please do not hesitate to call upon us. And thank you for flying ASA.

ATLANTA CONTROL: AC five twenty-nine, maintain one four thousand [14, 000 feet]. Contact Atlanta Center on 134.95.

In the next couple of minutes, Flight 529 climbs to 20,000 feet without incident, and the captain complains mildly about the repeated sounds of the altitude beeps. They have been flying now for nearly 21 minutes.

COCKPIT: [Sound of several thuds]

The torque on the left engine decreases to zero. The airplane rolls to the left, pitches down, and starts to descend at 5,500 feet per minute. In the cabin, the passengers hear a loud noise and the cabin shudders. Two of the three blades from the left propeller are wedged against the front of the wing. The Flight Attendant looked out the window and observed 'a mangled piece of machinery where the propeller and the front part of the cowling was'.

CAPTAIN: We got a left engine out. Left power lever. Flight idle.

COCKPIT: [A shaking sound starts and lasts for 33 seconds]

CAPTAIN: Left condition lever. Left condition lever.

CO-PILOT: Yeah.

CAPTAIN: Feather [propeller].

COCKPIT: [Series of beeps for one second indicating an engine fire]

CAPTAIN: Yeah, we're feathered. Left condition lever. Fuel shut-off. I need some help here.

CO-PILOT: Okay.

CAPTAIN: I need some help on this.

CO-PILOT: [You said the propeller is] feathered?

CAPTAIN: Uh.

CO-PILOT: It did feather.

CAPTAIN: It's feathered.

CO-PILOT: Okay.

CAPTAIN: What the hell's going on with this thing?

CO-PILOT: I don't know . . . [I] got this detector inop[erative].

CAPTAIN: Okay, let's put our headsets on. I can't hold this thing. Help me hold it.

CO-PILOT: Okay.

CAPTAIN: Okay, comin' on headset.

CO-PILOT: Atlanta Center. AC five twenty-nine, declaring an emergency. We've had an engine failure. We're out of fourteen [thousand] two [hundred] feet at this time.

CENTER: AC Five twenty-nine, roger. Left turn, direct Atlanta.

CAPTAIN: God damn.

COCKPIT: [Sound of heavy breathing]

CAPTAIN: All right. Turn your speaker off. Oh, we got it. It's . . . I pulled back, the power back.

CENTER: AC five twenty-nine, say altitude descending to.

CO-PILOT: We're out of eleven [thousand] six [hundred] at this time.

CAPTAIN: All right. It's . . . it's getting more controllable here. The engine . . . let's watch the speed. All right, We['re] trimmed completely here.

CO-PILOT: I'll tell Robin [the flight attendant] what's going on.

CO-PILOT TO FLIGHT ATTENDANT ON INTERPHONE: Okay, we had an engine failure, Robin. We declared an emergency. We're diverting back to Atlanta. Go ahead and, uh, brief the passengers. This will be an emergency landing back in . . .

FLIGHT ATTENDANT: All right, thank you.

CAPTAIN: Tell 'em we want . . .

ATLANTA CENTER: AC five twenty-nine, can you level off or do you need to keep descending?

CAPTAIN: [Tell 'em] we ca . . . We're gonna need to keep . . . descending. We need an airport quick.

CO-PILOT TO ATLANTA CENTER: Okay, we, uh, we're going to need to keep descending. We need an airport quick. Uh, roll the [emergency] trucks and everything for us.

ATLANTA CENTER: AC five twenty-nine, West Georgia, the regional airport is at your . . . ten o'clock position and about ten miles.

CO-PILOT: Understand – ten o'clock and ten miles.

CAPTAIN: Let's get the, uh, engine-failure checklist, please.

CO-PILOT [Getting the manual, paging through it]: Okay, I'll do it manually here. Okay, engine failure in flight. Power level's flight idle.

ATLANTA CENTER: AC five twenty-nine, you need to be on about a zero three zero heading for West Georgia Regional, sir.

CO-PILOT: Roger, we'll turn right. We're having, uh, difficulty controlling right now.

CO-PILOT [reading manual again]: Okay, condition lever's feather.

CAPTAIN: All right.

CO-PILOT [reading checklist]: Main auxiliary

generators of the failed engine off.

CAPTAIN: Okay, I got that.

CO-PILOT [reading]: APU [Auxiliary Power Unit] . . . if available, start. Want me to start it?

CAPTAIN: We gotta bring this down . . . bring those . . . Put that off.

ATLANTA CENTER: AC five twenty-nine, say your altitude now, sir.

CO-PILOT: Out of seven thousand . . .

CENTER: AC five twenty-nine, West Georgia Regional is your closest airport. The other one's, uh, Anniston. And that's about thirty miles to your west, sir.

CAPTAIN TO CO-PILOT: How long, how far [is] West Georgia Reg[ional]? What kind of runway they got?

CO-PILOT TO ATLANTA: What kind of runway's West Georgia Regional got?

CAPTAIN TO CO-PILOT: Go ahead and finish the check list.

ATLANTA: West Georgia Regional is, uh . . . it's five thousand feet [long].

CO-PILOT [going through the checklist]: Okay, APU started. Okay, prop sync, off. Prop sync's comin' off.

CAPTAIN: Okay.

CO-PILOT: Fuel pumps failed engine. You want, uh, max on this?

CAPTAIN: Go ahead, please.

CO-PILOT: Okay.

ATLANTA CENTER: And it is asphalt, sir.

CO-PILOT [continuing with checklist]: Hydraulic pump, failed engine? As required. Put it to the on position?

CAPTAIN: Correct.

CO-PILOT: Okay.

CAPTAIN: Okay.

CO-PILOT: Cross-bleed open.

CAPTAIN: Okay.

CO-PILOT: Electrical load, below four hundred amps.

CAPTAIN: It is . . . Well, you don't need to do that. Just leave that alone. All right, single-engine checklist, please.

ATLANTA CENTER: AC five twenty-nine, I've got you now and the airport's at your – say, say your heading now, sir.

CO-PILOT: Right now we're heading zero eight zero.

ATLANTA: Roger, you need about ten degrees left. [The airport] should be twelve o'clock and about eight miles.

CO-PILOT: Ten left, twelve 'n' eight miles, and, uh, do we got a ILS to this runway?

ATLANTA: Uh, I'll tell you what. Let me put you on Approach. He works that airport, and he will be able to give you more information. Contact Atlanta Approach on one two one point zero, sir.

CAPTAIN: We can get in [land] on a visual [approach without instruments].

ATLANTA: Good luck, guys.

CAPTAIN: Engine's exploded. It's just hanging out there.

ATLANTA APPROACH: AC five twenty-nine, Atlanta Approach.

CO-PILOT: Yes, sir. We're with you. Declaring an emergency.

CAPTAIN: We can get in on a visual. Just give us vectors [headings].

CO-PILOT TO ATLANTA APPROACH: Just give us vectors. We'll go the visual.

CAPTAIN TO CO-PILOT: Sing, single, single-engine check list, please.

CO-PILOT: Where the hell is it [the checklist]?

ATLANTA: AC five twenty-nine, say altitude leaving.

CO-PILOT: We're out of nineteen hundred [1,900] at this time.

CAPTAIN: We're below the clouds. Tell 'em . . .

CO-PILOT TO ATLANTA: Okay, we're, uh, VFR at this time. Give us a vector to the airport.

ATLANTA: AC five twenty-nine, turn left, uh, fly heading zero four zero . . . The airport's at your, about ten o'clock and six miles, sir. Radar contact lost [at] this time.

COCKPIT: [Mechanical voice] *Five hundred* [feet]. *Too low gear.*

ATLANTA: AC Five twenty-nine, if able, change to my frequency, one one eight point seven. The airport, uh, [is] in the vicinity of your ten o'clock at twelve o'clock and about four miles or so.

CAPTAIN TO CO-PILOT: Help me. Help me hold it. Help me hold it. Help me hold it.

COCKPIT: [Vibrating sound as the stick shaker starts warning of stall]

CO-PILOT: Amy, I love you.

COCKPIT: [Sound of grunting]

COCKPIT: [Sound of impact]

END OF TAPE

While the Flight Attendant was preparing the passengers for an emergency landing, she looked out of the window and saw treetops. She had already checked with each passenger to see whether they understood how to brace themselves against impact, and as she took her own seat and belted herself in, she yelled instructions to the passengers until the time of impact.

The airplane sheared off several trees along a path 360 feet long before hitting the ground along a slight upslope. The airplane came to rest 850 feet from where it first hit the trees.

On impact, overhead storage bins fell down and the seats were torn from their anchors on the cabin floor. As the airplane slid on its left side, holes large enough to see through were punched in the fuselage.

About a minute after the airplane came to a stop, crackling sounds and sparks from electrical wires preceded a fire which quickly engulfed the cabin. Spilled aviation fuel saturated some of the passengers' clothing, and one passenger saw 'a couple of people on fire'.

None of the passengers escaped through the exit doors. Those who could manage escaped through the holes in the fuselage.

Despite second-degree burns to her ankles and legs, the Flight Attendant ran through the flames to help passengers out of the aircraft. She put out the flames on at least one person who was on fire.

The Co-pilot tried to open the right cockpit window, which was damaged by the impact. He could not get out of the cockpit door. He chopped a hole in the cockpit window with a small axe. He handed the axe out the hole to a passenger, who chopped at the window but could not make a hole large enough for the Co-pilot to exit through. A continuous roar of fire was heard in the cockpit from behind the cockpit door.

The Co-pilot and Captain were trapped.

Five minutes after the crash, the local fire department arrived. When firemen could not smash through the cockpit window with larger axes, they poured water in the hole to control the fire that was burning in the cockpit. Once they extinguished the flames in the cabin, they rescued the Co-pilot through the cockpit door. The Captain was already dead of burns and smoke inhalation. The Co-pilot suffered burns over 80 per cent of his body.

The Captain and seven passengers died. The Co-pilot, the Flight Attendant and 19 passengers survived the crash of Flight 529.

This incident presaged a disaster years later in the crash of the Valujet in the Everglades (see Chapter 24). On 3 February 1988, a spontaneous chemical fire smouldered out of sight in the cargo hold of American Airlines Flight 132. On final approach to land, the cabin floor was softening, sinking and simply melting under tremendous heat. A deadheading Co-pilot riding in the passenger cabin who observed the floor told the Co-pilot in the cockpit, '[We're] gonna have to land this thing in a hurry'.

Until this moment, the flight was nothing but routine.

A McDonnell Douglas DC-9, Flight 132 had departed Dallas–Fort Worth at 2.45 that afternoon destined for Nashville. There were 120 passengers, four flight attendants, and two deadheading flight crew members aboard. The cargo holds contained 6,365 pounds of air freight. There was a 20-pound cylinder of oxygen and a 104-pound drum of textile treatment chemicals, including five gallons of hydrogen peroxide solution, an oxidizer and 25 pounds of a sodium orthosilicate-based mixture, which is a granular solid material. No labels marked the drum to indicate the hazards of its contents. The oxygen cylinder and the drum were put in the middle cargo hold; the drum was laid on its side.

We pick up the CVR tape just as the Flight Attendant is telling the cockpit about the fire.

CO-PILOT [speaks in interphone to back of the aircraft]: Hello.

FLIGHT ATTENDANT [calling the cockpit on interphone from back of the aircraft]: Hi. We've got smoke in the cabin.

CO-PILOT: Okay.

FLIGHT ATTENDANT: We don't know where it's coming from. It's past the, ah, exit. [We] got an H_2O extinguisher . . .

APPROACH CONTROL: American one thirty-two, descend and maintain two thousand five-hundred [feet].

CAPTAIN: Two thousand five-hundred, American one thirty-two.

CO-PILOT TO CAPTAIN: We got smoke in the . . . ah . . .

FLIGHT ATTENDANT: It's a real bad smell.

CO-PILOT TO FLIGHT ATTENDANT: Okay, I smell it up here now.

CO-PILOT TO CAPTAIN: [They] smell smoke. [They] got smoke in the cabin.

CAPTAIN: Smoke, or . . .

CO-PILOT: It smells electrical.

CAPTAIN: Fumes.

CO-PILOT: They can't tell where it's coming from. It smells electrical.

CAPTAIN: Is it fumes or smoke?

FLIGHT ATTENDANT: Yeah, a pilot [deadheading Co-pilot who was riding in the passenger cabin] said the floor is getting really soft, and he said we need to land.

CO-PILOT: Okay. Who says the floor is getting soft?

FLIGHT ATTENDANT: Here he is [handing the interphone to the deadheading Co-pilot].

DEADHEAD CO-PILOT: Hey, boss.

CO-PILOT: Yes?

DEADHEAD: You got the floor back here in the middle . . . dropping out slightly.

CO-PILOT: Okay.

DEADHEAD: You[re] gonna have to land this thing in a hurry.

CO-PILOT: Okay, we're gettin' it down now.

DEADHEAD: Okay, be quick.

Co-PILOT: Okay.

DEADHEAD: Hey, have the [fire] trucks meet us [once we land].

CO-PILOT TO CAPTAIN: [We] have a flight officer back there, says that the floor is getting soft. [We] probably ought to drop the [landing] gear. There's somethin' going on in the, ah, floor board.

CAPTAIN: Put the gear down.

COCKPIT: [Sound of landing gear being lowered]

CO-PILOT TO FLIGHT ATTENDANT: Okay, now how far back is the floor getting soft?

FLIGHT ATTENDANT: Well, ah, the Captain [deadheading Co-pilot] is in the aisle right now. He's about midway through to . . .

CO-PILOT: About where the [landing] gear might be?

FLIGHT ATTENDANT: Yes.

CO-PILOT: Okay. Why don't you go back and buckle in.

FLIGHT ATTENDANT: We're all seated.

CO-PILOT: Okay, fine. [Then to Captain] Okay, what do you want me to do here? Okay, seatbelt [sign] . . .

CAPTAIN: Yes.

CO-PILOT: No smoking sign . . .

CAPTAIN: No smoke. Just fumes, right?

CO-PILOT: So far it's just smoke . . . fumes.

[Now to Flight Attendant on interphone] You don't see any smoke. It's just fumes?

FLIGHT ATTENDANT: Bad fumes. Startin' to hurt my eyes.

CO-PILOT: Okay. I'm gonna get off the phone. Call me if anything important changes.

FLIGHT ATTENDANT: Okay.

CAPTAIN TO CO-PILOT: Did you call the Tower?

NASHVILLE TOWER: American one thirty-two, Nashville Tower. Wind calm [on] Runway Two left. Cleared to land.

CAPTAIN: No problems.

CO-PILOT: There's just fumes back there.

CAPTAIN: We've had fumes before, from the APU [Auxiliary Power Unit] is where [it came from] at least initially. Okay, we got [landing] gear.

CO-PILOT: Gear.

CAPTAIN: Spoiler lever, auto brakes. No. Flaps are good. Lights. Are we cleared to land?

CO-PILOT TO TOWER: American one thirty-two, are we cleared to land?

TOWER: Affirmative.

CO-PILOT: Roger. [To Captain] Do you want to call any . . . [emergency equipment on the ground]?

CAPTAIN: We don't have any problems yet. Just a few fumes.

CO-PILOT: You don't smell it?

CAPTAIN: Yeah, I smell it.

CO-PILOT: You are cleared to land. Landing checklist is complete. Five hundred feet, sinkin' a thousand plus five. Four hundred [feet]. Three hundred [feet]. There's two hundred. one hundred. On the tape, fifty, forty, thirty, ten, five . . .

COCKPIT: Sound of touchdown

CO-PILOT: Reverse [thrust]. Hundred knots. Eighty knots.

TOWER: American one thirty-two, turn right. When able contact ground control.

CO-PILOT: Sixty knots.

GROUND CONTROL: American one thirty-two, Nashville ground. Roger, your option [is] to enter Tango Two [runway exit] or come down to Tango Four. Advise.

CO-PILOT: Tango Two or Tango Four.

CAPTAIN: Ah, let's see . . .

CO-PILOT: This is my first time in here, so let me look this up.

COCKPIT: [Sound of cabin chimes with flight attendant calling cockpit]

CO-PILOT: I'm here.

DEADHEAD CO-PILOT ON INTERPHONE: You've got a big problem back here, and

I'm not sure if you . . . The problem is, I don't know where the heat is comin' from. It's comin' up through the floor.

CO-PILOT: Do you see any smoke?

DEADHEAD: Yeah, there's smoke. Just a little bit.

CO-PILOT: Okay, okay.

DEADHEAD: We better get outta here.

CO-PILOT: Okay.

FLIGHT ATTENDANT TO CAPTAIN: Ah, Captain?

CO-PILOT TO CAPTAIN: There's a crew[man] back there that says we better get outta here. He says there's smoke comin' through the floor.

FLIGHT ATTENDANT: I don't see it [the smoke]. We had a first officer here with us. He's the one. He's been checkin' the floor. He's in uniform. That's who you've been talkin' to . . .

CO-PILOT TO CAPTAIN: She don't see [the smoke].

FLIGHT ATTENDANT: He [the deadhead Co-pilot] thinks it's real soft, the floor's real soft.

CO-PILOT TO CAPTAIN: The floor is getting very very soft.

CAPTAIN: Okay, let's get out of here. Call ground . . .

CO-PILOT TO FLIGHT ATTENDANT: Okay, we're gonna get out of the airplane now.

FLIGHT ATTENDANT. Okay, Easy Victor [evacuation].

CO-PILOT: Ah, stand by.

FLIGHT ATTENDANT: Okay.

CAPTAIN: Give me the checklist.

CO-PILOT TO GROUND CONTROL: Ah, roger, sir, would you call out the fire equipment? We've got the possibility of some fire, some real hot stuff, in the cargo compartment. The floor is real hot. We're gonna get 'em [the passengers] out.

GROUND CONTROL: Okay, we got 'em on the phone, American one thirty-two.

CO-PILOT TO CAPTAIN: Okay, ground evac. Ah, Tower. Called the Tower. Flaps.

CAPTAIN: [Flaps] Forty [fully extended].

CAPTAIN: Spoiler lever . . .

CAPTAIN: You get out of here. You go help [the Flight Attendants]. Retract brakes. Park fuel levers.

CO-PILOT: Cut-off

END OF TAPE

The Captain ordered the evacuation two minutes and six seconds after Flight 132 touched down, and the inflatable slides were deployed at the two forward cabin doors, the aft galley door and in the tail cone. The overwing exits were not used. No instructions were given to the passengers over the public address system. Neither were they prepared for the evacuation before landing. During the evacuation, the flight attendants shouted commands at the passengers to 'Unfasten seat belts' and 'Come this way' and 'Remove shoes' and 'Don't take anything with you.'

After the passengers had safely evacuated the airplane, an American Airlines maintenance employee on the ground asked the Captain about the problem. The Captain said there was a fire in the cargo area. They opened the aft cargo compartment and saw little smoke inside. Then they opened the middle cargo compartment. Thick, white/grey smoke poured out.

The Tower's call dispatched 14 firefighters with six vehicles, four crash-fire rescue units and two quick response units to the aircraft, which had pulled to a stop on the apron beside the runway. The emergency units sprayed about 120 gallons of water into the middle cargo compartment to douse the smouldering fires. Neither aqueous film-forming foam nor dry chemicals to fight fires was used.

None of the 126 crew and passengers was injured seriously; nine passengers and four crew suffered minor injuries.

This was a flight no one would have chosen to take off, not because any of the 27 passengers and three crew members were killed or even injured, but because the twin-engined propeller Brazilian Embraer EMB-120 RT stalled suddenly while climbing to its flight altitude at 17,000 feet and plummeted to 5,500 feet before the crew regained control. Then, with one of the two engines badly damaged and with three of the four propeller blades missing, the airplane could not maintain level flight. In other words, it was going down and only an airport nearby could save them. The crew could have avoided the whole incident if the Pilot had not been – in the characterization of the National Transportation Safety Board – so 'relaxed'.

Continental Airlines Continental Express Flight 2733 (called Jet Link 2733) left Little Rock, Arkansas, en route to Houston, Texas, in the middle of the afternoon. The flight was instructed to climb through 7,500 feet and maintain a flight level of 22,000 feet. The weather was overcast with a visibility of nearly five miles, temperature of 68₁ F, light winds, and moderate icing in the clouds and precipitation between 12,000 and 20,000 feet. In other words, the weather was good for flying.

After take-off and while climbing, the Co-pilot wrote in his log book and ate his in-flight meal. The Captain, who had a reputation for being 'easy to get along with', loosened his safety harness and put his foot up on the console, according to one passenger who was watching through the open door. The Flight Attendant had made her way forward and was standing in the door chatting with the Captain, who had put the aircraft on auto-pilot. The crew had spent the morning and early part of the afternoon together poolside at the motel where they were staying in Little Rock.

We will begin the tape transcript during take-off.

TOWER: Jet Link twenty-seven thirty-three [you are] cleared for take-off [on runway]. Two two Right. Turn left [after take-off on] heading one eight zero.

CO-PILOT: Turn left [to] one eight zero, cleared to go [on] Two two Right, twenty-seven thirty-three.

COCKPIT: [Sound of increasing engine noise as throttles were pushed forward]

CO-PILOT: [Throttles] Set. Eight [mph]. Vee one. Vee two. Positive rate.

CAPTAIN: [Landing] Gear up.

CO-PILOT: Acceleration.

CAPTAIN: Okay, flaps [up].

TOWER: Jet Link twenty-seven thirty-three, contact departure.

CO-PILOT: Twenty-seven thirty-three, so long. Departure, Jet Link twenty-seven thirty-three's with you [on radio frequency] one point three, [flying at] four thousand [feet], [at a heading of] one eight zero heading.

DEPARTURE: Jet Link twenty-seven thirty-three . . . maintain one zero [10,000] thousand.

CAPTAIN: What do you think you're doin'?

CO-PILOT: I don't know.

For the next few minutes or so Flight 2733 continues to climb through clouds, with the Co-pilot contacting Little Rock Departure and Memphis Center for heading and altitude instructions. The Co-pilot tells the Captain that he is going to run some calculations to see whether a flight altitude of 26,000 feet might not be better for them than the assigned 22,000 feet.

CO-PILOT: I'm gonna go ahead and run a weight for two six oh right [26,000 feet].

CAPTAIN: I don't . . . I don't care. I don't know what the winds are like up there [at 26,000 feet].

The Flight Attendant, while the aircraft is still climbing, comes to the cockpit door.

FLIGHT ATTENDANT: Hi.

CAPTAIN TO CO-PILOT: Not much difference [in the winds], huh?

CO-PILOT: At eighteen [thousand feet], it's, ah, two ninety at twenty-six, at two four [24,000 feet] it's twenty-six at thirty-three.

CAPTAIN: [The flight altitude between 22,000 and 26,000] It really don't make a big difference.

CO-PILOT: The higher you go . . .

CAPTAIN: . . . The more it turns into a headwind, anyway.

CO-PILOT: Yeah. What do you want to go for a final [cruising altitude]? You want to go [to 26,000 feet]?

CAPTAIN: I don't care.

The Flight Attendant asks if the Captain and the Co-pilot want to eat. The Co-pilot says he does, the Captain says, 'No, no thanks.' And the Flight Attendant leaves the cockpit momentarily to get the meal for the Co-pilot.

CAPTAIN [to Co-pilot and Flight Attendant]: Do you guys really want to eat somethin' that bad?
CO-PILOT TO CAPTAIN: That girl has got you all screwed up . . . It looks like [you can't] concentrate.

The Captain apparently has been put on a diet by 'that girl', and he is worried about maintaining his diet.

CAPTAIN: Man, I just couldn't help it. I was tryin'. I was tryin' to change the conversation, all right.
CO-PILOT: Yeah.
CENTER: Jet Link twenty-seven thirty-three, climb and maintain flight level 23,000 [feet]
CAPTAIN: When I get back to [one hundred] eighty-five [pounds].
CO-PILOT: Eighty-five.

Now, the Co-pilot and the Captain engage in a bit of banter, and when the Flight Attendant comes back into the cockpit, she and the Captain take up the conversation, now about a bug that is stuck on the windshield of the aircraft.

FLIGHT ATTENDANT TO CAPTAIN: Oh, do the windshield wipers. That'll wipe it [the bug] off.
CAPTAIN: Naw. I can't. Naw. I can't do it 'cause we're goin' too fast.
FLIGHT ATTENDANT: That'd be funny. That'd be funny. That'd crack me up. That'll make my day.
CAPTAIN: Off.
FLIGHT ATTENDANT: Do it, do it, do it.
CAPTAIN: Okay.
FLIGHT ATTENDANT: Can't we climb any faster?
CAPTAIN: Why do you want to get up so fast?
FLIGHT ATTENDANT: I can't pull it uphill.

The Flight Attendant wants the Captain to reach cruise altitude faster because she does not want to have to push the drinks cart up the aisle while the airplane is still in a climb attitude.

CAPTAIN: Okay.

FLIGHT ATTENDANT: The last time I had to pull it up the hill [aisle].

CAPTAIN: We'll try to get up a little more [a little faster].

FLIGHT ATTENDANT: We'll try to get up there?

CAPTAIN: Yeah. We're almost there [to cruise altitude]. Another six thousand feet, another six minutes.

Here the Flight Attendant fools with the Captain. She offers him something that the tape does not make clear.

FLIGHT ATTENDANT: Gimme, gimme, gimme. Climb. Gimme, gimme, gimme.

CAPTAIN TO FLIGHT ATTENDANT: You're right. Better to receive than to give.

FLIGHT ATTENDANT: What?

CAPTAIN: Ah, like you said. Better to receive than to give.

FLIGHT ATTENDANT: I don't know.

CAPTAIN: [I] Live by that.

The Captain and the Flight Attendant engage in another five seconds of what the NTSB calls 'non pertinent' conversation.

CAPTAIN: We're not climbin' very fast. Yeah, we're really heavy.

At this point, ice was starting to form on the wings and the improper instructions that the Captain gave to the auto-pilot for flight vertical mode are making the airplane unstable. Its 'heaviness' is the indication that it is about to stall.

FLIGHT ATTENDANT: I know . . . I know [I couldn't, or you couldn't] walk, like walk a straight line, [and] not sway all over it.

CAPTAIN: [Laughs]

FLIGHT ATTENDANT: [Laughs] So that's what you meant by a weight problem.

CAPTAIN TO CO-PILOT: Frank, hang on. This ain't right.

Two seconds go by, and the stall-indicating stick shaker starts to shake the control yoke, and the auto-pilot automatically disconnects. The airplane plummets. The Flight Attendant is thrown back into the passenger cabin. During the ensuing descent – freefall of the airplane – the Flight Attendant yells to the passengers to assume 'impact' position; she tells them the location of the emergency exits. She tells them that their landing will be 'hard and fast'.

CAPTAIN: Airspeed.
COCKPIT: [Stall warning sounds]
CAPTAIN: Hang on. Hang on. Power's up . . . power's . . .
COCKPIT: [Sound of increasing engine noise]
CAPTAIN: Up . . .

Here the Captain pulls back hard on the control column, making the recovery of the airplane more difficult to achieve as it falls nearly 12,000 feet.

COCKPIT: [Sound of vibration]
CAPTAIN: Up . . . I think it's an overspeed. It's an overspeed.

END OF TAPE

As the tape ended, the Captain shut down the left engine, which he thought was racing out of control, when in fact it was badly damaged. The Co-pilot lowered the landing gear, which helped them to regain control of the airplane, and the crew declared an emergency, stating that they needed to land 'immediately and were losing altitude'. The Captain decided to make the emergency landing at Pine Bluff airport. Five minutes before Flight 2733 reached the airport, the Pine Bluff airport manager ordered Runway 17 cleared of construction equipment. Flight 2733 broke out of the clouds about one mile from the end of the runway. The Captain overshot the runway and touched down with 1,880 feet of runway remaining. He applied the brakes but the runway was wet, and the airplane 'hydroplaned' or skidded off the asphalt surface onto the grass, narrowly missing a construction vehicle and several construction workers who were watching at the time. The airplane came to a rest 687 feet from the end of Runway 17. The crew and passengers immediately evacuated. There was only one minor injury. The NTSB determined that the probable causes of the incident were 'the Captain's failure to maintain professional cockpit discipline, his consequent inattention to flight instruments and ice accretion, and his selection of an improper auto-flight vertical mode, all of which led to an aerodynamic stall, loss of control, and a forced landing'.

As they taxied out for take-off from Alaska International Airport, en route to Chicago–O'Hare, the crew of Japan Airlines' cargo Flight 46E was warned of severe turbulence, and later, just before take-off, they were told that a flight departing ahead of them had experienced severe turbulence at 2,500 feet while climbing out from Runway 6R. Notice the differences and similarities between this flight and El Al 1862 (see Chapter 10): the same kind of airplane with the same catastrophic failure.

Flight 46E was a Boeing 747–121 loaded with cargo with a crew that consisted of a Captain, Co-pilot, Flight Engineer, and two company employees along for the ride. Other aircraft in the area or at the airport are Japan Airlines 42E and Peninsula 4205.

We pick up the CVR just as the flight is taxiing out for take-off.

FLIGHT ENGINEER: You gotta' get your priorities right.
CAPTAIN: Yeah, right. What'd you come up here for?

FLIGHT ENGINEER: This is [the best angle or view] right here that I can see.

The Flight Engineer apparently is taking a photograph out of the cockpit window of two airplanes that are taking-off ahead of them.

CO-PILOT: [Try to] get both of them in the same picture.
ENGINEER: I am.
COCKPIT: [Sound of laughter]
CAPTAIN: Do it.
ENGINEER: Oh, yeah, I got it, actually.
COCKPIT: [Sound of laughter]
ENGINEER: Oh, I got it twice. That's cool. I didn't even see what you're talking about. I won't get the rotate but those are good pictures. Actually I got more of the little guy than I had of our plane, but it's kinda neat for comparison.
CAPTAIN: Fun stuff, huh?
ENGINEER: Really. Okay, uh, let's see, where were we? We did, uh, stab[ilizer] trim, then we did INS [Inertial Navigation System]. How about pitot heat?

CO-PILOT: On.

TOWER: Japan Air forty-six heavy, contact departure.

ENGINEER: Fuel heat's checked and off. Anti-ice?

CO-PILOT: Checked and off.

ENGINEER: Shoulder harness?

CAPTAIN: On.

CO-PILOT: On.

ENGINEER: Comin' on. Take-off brief?

CO-PILOT: Understood.

CAPTAIN: Same brief as before. Ah, the departure is still eleven miles, two thousand feet, three hundred and thirty degree heading, going two zero zero. Okay?

ENGINEER: Yup. Understood. Flight instruments?

CAPTAIN: Checked.

CO-PILOT: Checked.

ENGINEER: Taxi check complete. That was a cool picture though. I didn't even see the other guy comin' and I was just looking because all I saw was the little tube, you know, and, uh, and what I saw [in] my view finder. All of a sudden he came in there and . . . there's a [C-] one four one piece of crap or a C-five, one of the two.

CO-PILOT: Are you still flying those?

ENGINEER: Yeah, I hate 'em.

CAPTAIN: [It's called a] Skylifter.

ENGINEER: It's gross. The whole air conditioning system stinks. [When you] get off the airplane you smell like a [C-] one four one. Yeah, that's what it is.

CAPTAIN: [Somebody] had a model of a one four one in there and on the box it said 'Sky lizard'.

ENGINEER: Did it really? Okay, flaps, Vee speeds, trim?

CAPTAIN: Re-checked for Six right.

CO-PILOT: Re-checked for Six right.

ENGINEER: Checked. [Six right] for take-off. Six right anti-ice? Off, INS?

CAPTAIN: Checked.

ENGINEER: APU goin' off. Fuel system set for take-off. Forty-two Echo said expect a rough ride.

CO-PILOT: Japan Air, forty-six Echo heavy is ready.

TOWER: Japan Air forty-six Echo heavy Anchorage tower Runway Six right, taxi into position and hold. Pilot reports severe turbulence leaving two thousand five hundred . . .

CAPTAIN: Okay.

CO-PILOT: Roger, understood. Thank you.

ENGINEER: Batten down the hatches, folks. We're expecting a rough ride.

TOWER: Japan Air forty-six Echo heavy, Runway Six right, cleared for take-off.

ENGINEER: [Reports of] severe turbulence on climb out. I don't what else is out on that galley now, but we're getting ready to blast off, so just keep an eye out.

CAPTAIN: All the way on the check list.

ENGINEER: All the way.

CAPTAIN: Cleared to go.

The crew completes its before take-off checklist.

COCKPIT: [Sound of engine power increasing]

CAPTAIN: Max power.

ENGINEER: Max power. Max power is set, and you've got . . . ninety-three per cent.

CAPTAIN: Thanks.

CO-PILOT: Eighty knots. Vee One. Rotate. Vee Two. Positive rate.

CAPTAIN: Gear up.

TOWER: Japan Air, forty-six Echo heavy, contact departure.

CO-PILOT: Good day.

DEPARTURE: Japan Air forty-six Echo heavy, turn right heading three five zero.

CO-PILOT: Good afternoon, Japan Air forty-six Echo, out of one thousand for two zero zero.

DEPARTURE: Japan Air forty-six Echo heavy, Anchorage departure, radar contact, expect severe turbulence [at] two thousand five hundred, heavy seven-four-seven, smooth to moderate, continuous moderate [at] three thousand through one zero thousand.

CO-PILOT: Roger.

CAPTAIN: Max climb power.

ENGINEER: Max climb.

Now, the Boeing 747 enters the area of severe turbulence.

ENGINEER: Hang on guys.

CO-PILOT: Left three three zero.

CAPTAIN: Flaps five.

CO-PILOT: Flaps five.

CAPTAIN: Flaps up.

ENGINEER: Flaps up. Whoa, whoa, whoa.

COCKPIT: [Sound of snap and sound of warning horn]

The violent turbulence throws the Boeing 747 into a severe banking turn of approximately 50°. While the desired air speed was 183 knots, the air speed fluctuated about 75 knots from a high of 245 knots to a low of 170 knots. The No. 2 throttle slammed to its aft stop, and the No. 2 thrust reverser showed deployment. The airplane pitched and rolled severely before the engine separated from the wing.

ENGINEER: Whoa, whoa, thrust reverser . . . We got auto fail. We lost something.

CO-PILOT: [We] lost number one and two [engines].

CAPTAIN: [Number] two's gone.

ENGINEER: Number two engine shut down. Whoa, whoa.

COCKPIT: [*Bank angle, bank angle*]

CAPTAIN: All right. [Declare an] emergency.

ENGINEER: Number two start levers cut-off.

ANCHORAGE DEPARTURE: Japan Air forty-six Echo heavy, ah, Elmendorf Tower said that something large just fell off your airplane.

CAPTAIN: Yeah, we know it.

CO-PILOT TO ANCHORAGE TOWER: We know that ah, we're ah, declaring an emergency.

DEPARTURE: Japan Air forty-six Echo heavy, will you need to return to Anchorage?

CAPTAIN: We are returning to . . .

Shortly after the engine separated from the airplane, the flightcrew declared an emergency and the Captain initiated a large radius turn to the left to return and land on Anchorage International's Runway 6R. Maximum power was applied to the No. 1 engine. As it maneuvered for landing approach, the bank angles of the Boeing 747 exceeded 40°.

CO-PILOT: Standby. Returning. And we are declaring an emergency.

DEPARTURE: Japan Air forty-six Echo heavy, turn left heading two four zero. Maintain three thousand, vector ILS Runway Six right final approach course.

COCKPIT: [*Bank angle, bank angle*]

ENGINEER: Okay, hang on. Do you wanna dump fuel?

CO-PILOT: Standby one, standby one. We've got an airplane comin' to us.

ENGINEER: Verify number two fire handle.

CAPTAIN: Yes, sir, there's traffic ten o'clock, two miles, three thousand eight hundred, climbing rapidly.

COCKPIT: [Sound of warning horn]

CAPTAIN: We got traffic over . . .

ENGINEER: Number two, verify, fire handle.

DEPARTURE: Japan Air four-six Echo heavy, that traffic's leaving five thousand five hundred.

CO-PILOT: Number two [fire handle] set.

ENGINEER: We're turning back [to] Anchorage. We got two leading edge devices out on the left side.

DEPARTURE: Japan Air four-six Echo heavy, descend and maintain one thousand six hundred. Can you use Runway One four? It's closer.

CAPTAIN: You dumping fuel?

CO-PILOT TO DEPARTURE: Roger, standby one please.

ENGINEER TO CAPTAIN: Not yet . . . need some help up here.

CAPTAIN: Okay, now. Okay, give me [the] flaps back.

CO-PILOT: Five, five?

CAPTAIN: Five.

CO-PILOT: Flaps coming five.

ENGINEER: Okay, fuel's comin' off. Okay, flaps are comin' down. Number two engine's secured. Fuel dumping is in progress. You wanna dump down to five eighty-five, correct?

CAPTAIN: We're gonna, well, I'm having a real hard . . .

CO-PILOT: I think we lost the engine.

ENGINEER: We lost number two engine.

DEPARTURE: Japan Air four-six Echo heavy, say your intentions.

ENGINEER: [We need] thirty minutes [to] dump [fuel].

CO-PILOT: We, we are ah, we are going to maintain this heading to, ah . . . we are having problems with our flight controls, and also, ah, speed. Standby one.

CAPTAIN: Everybody secured?

ENGINEER: Everybody's secured.

DEPARTURE: Roger, any runway, Japan Air four-six Echo heavy. Ah, any runway you need.

ENGINEER: Tell me what kinda' gross, what kinda' fuel weight that is. [I gotta find] zero fuel [weight].

CAPTAIN: Are you dumping fuel?

ENGINEER: Yes, we are. Would you like the quick return?

CAPTAIN: Quick return to the line please.

ENGINEER: Okay, quick return, to the line. Landing gear?

CO-PILOT: Off, uh . . .

CAPTAIN: Off.

ENGINEER: You got all but number two [engine], number three is down, it's in progress. Okay, quick return. Landing gear?

CO-PILOT: Ah, up, a . . .

ENGINEER: Flaps?

CO-PILOT: Flaps are maintaining five degrees.

ENGINEER: Five degrees . . . Speed brake handle?

CO-PILOT: [Forward]

CAPTAIN: Did you declare an emergency for us?

DEPARTURE: Japan Air four-six Echo heavy, are you able to maintain terrain clearance?

CO-PILOT: Affirmative at this time, and ah, we are maintaining, ah, thirteen hundred [feet].

DEPARTURE: Japan Air four-six Echo heavy, roger.

CO-PILOT: We are dumping fuel.

DEPARTURE: Japan Air four-six Echo heavy, roger.

ENGINEER: Okay.

CAPTAIN: You did declare an emergency?

CO-PILOT: Yes, affirmative.

CAPTAIN: Give me some speeds quickly.

ENGINEER: Okay, speeds gonna be . . . for five eighty-five, I believe one forty-five [mph].

CAPTAIN: All right. How's our weight doing?

ENGINEER: I'll get it to you in a second. Don't have time to do it perfect.

CAPTAIN: Give me, ah, ILS on the, ah, radios.

ENGINEER: What was the fuel weight that you came up with? We need it now.

CAPTAIN: We're gonna lose number, number one [engine] here for temperatures.

COCKPIT: [Sound of warning horn]

DEPARTURE: Japan Air four-six heavy, I have two F-fifteens off your fight wing three miles, they have you visually, and if you'd like any panel inspection they said they [can] get in closer and, ah, and look you over.

CAPTAIN: Yeah, [tell them to] go ahead.

CO-PILOT: Go ahead.

DEPARTURE TO FIGHTER JETS: Lion One, they said, ah, you can proceed on in and take a look and see how much damage has been done.

ENGINEER: Okay.

CO-PILOT TO CAPTAIN: Okay, which runway do you want?

CAPTAIN: [We're gonna] want [Runway] Six right.

CO-PILOT TO DEPARTURE: We'd like the Runway Six right, this is ah, Japan Air forty-six Echo.

ENGINEER: In-flight failure check, shutdown check is complete.

CAPTAIN: Why am I losing air speed here?

DEPARTURE: Japan Air four-six Echo heavy,

understand turning inbound to Runway Six right.

ENGINEER: What's the airspeed?

COCKPIT: [Recorded altitude warning: *One thousand feet*]

CO-PILOT: You want, ah, some ah, some, rudder trim? Rudder trim?

CAPTAIN: That's not gonna help. Let's try to get this thing turned around.

ENGINEER: These numbers are wrong. One forty-five, one fifty-one. I don't know, it's back here [someplace]. [I had a] piece of paper . . . No, [I mean on, like, departure, I had] that fuel oil schedule.

CAPTAIN: I just want to stay out of the water here, you guys.

CO-PILOT: Okay.

CAPTAIN: Emergency power.

CO-PILOT: Okay, I got it.

CAPTAIN: Flaps. Well no we can't.

CO-PILOT: You want flaps?

CAPTAIN: No.

ENGINEER: Hundred feet . . . fuel weight of seven hundred, right now.

CAPTAIN: How much [is] the airplane weigh?

ENGINEER: The airplane right now weighs seven hundred, your Vee speeds for flaps thirty . . . ref speed is . . . one sixty-three . . . Vee ref.

CAPTAIN: How much does the airplane weigh?

ENGINEER: I'm showin' it weighs six eighty seven, right now. [There's] fuel dumping in progress.

CAPTAIN: [We will have] to land heavy.

ENGINEER: Okay, land heavy, heavy weight landing for . . .

DEPARTURE: Understand, ah, he's lost the ah, left [flap] on the left wing?

CO-PILOT: We got a fighter [jet] over out, over here. He's looking at, he's looking at us, yeah.

CAPTAIN: All right, we're going to get [no] left flap. All right, quick return, below the line.

DEPARTURE: Japan Air four-six Echo heavy, you've lost, ah, approximately fifty per cent of the leading edge slats on the left wing, and structural damage to the trailing edge flaps.

CAPTAIN: All right.

CO-PILOT: You want to land [on this runway]?

CAPTAIN: I want to land on that runway, right now.

CO-PILOT: You want flaps, more flaps?

DEPARTURE: Japan Air four-six Echo heavy, runway six right, cleared to land.

CAPTAIN: All right. All right. We're landing . . .

CO-PILOT: We're on [Runway] six left.

CAPTAIN: Discontinue dump[ing of fuel].

ENGINEER: All right, discontinuing dump. And you want gear down?

CO-PILOT: Okay, slow down. You can slow down now.

CAPTAIN: Gear down.

CO-PILOT: Gear down?

COCKPIT: [*Glideslope*]

DEPARTURE: Japan Air four-six Echo Heavy, did you copy the wind shear report, sir?

ENGINEER: Landing gear and tilt?

CO-PILOT: Okay, do you want more flap, or flap five is okay?

CAPTAIN: We're gonna go . . .

ENGINEER: Landing gear tilt, down and green.

CO-PILOT TO DEPARTURE: Roger, we copy. We are coming for Runway Six right.

COCKPIT: [*Glideslope, glideslope*]

DEPARTURE: Japan Air forty-six Echo heavy, all the gear appears to be good.

CO-PILOT TO DEPARTURE: Thank you.

ENGINEER: You got ADF on both, flight instruments, radio no flags, air condit . . .

COCKPIT: [*Terrain, terrain*]

CAPTAIN: Zero trim.

CO-PILOT: Two hundred feet. Zero the trim.

ENGINEER: Speed brake handle.

CAPTAIN: Flaps twenty-five.

CO-PILOT: Flaps are comin' twenty-five. Flaps is twenty-five.

COCKPIT: [*One hundred* (feet) *fifty* (feet) *thirty* (feet)]

ENGINEER: Before landing checklist complete.

COCKPIT: Twenty [feet]. . . . ten [feet].

ENGINEER: Hang on guys. Spoilers extended, reverse available one two three [engines], or one three four [engines].

DEPARTURE TO FIGHTER JETS: Lion One, advise when he's down. Lion One, wilco and thank you for the assistance.

CAPTAIN: Thank you.

ENGINEER: Thank you. I can't see your speed so, uh . . .

CO-PILOT: Ninety [mph].

ENGINEER: Eighty knots.

CAPTAIN: Tell that guy thanks for his help.

ENGINEER: That's cool. Okay, we've got thrust reverser, lights out.

CAPTAIN: All right, secure . . .

CO-PILOT: Ah, thank you very much Tower,

this is Evergreen, ah, Japan Air forty-six Echo. Thank the fighters for us.

DEPARTURE: Japan Air four-six Echo heavy, and ah, they [the fighters] wish to say you did a good job and, ah, thank you.

ENGINEER: [Laughter]

DEPARTURE: Japan Air four-six Echo heavy, contact Anchorage ground one two one point niner.

CO-PILOT: Thank you and roger, good day.

ENGINEER TO CO-PILOT: Thanks, buddy. I don't care how much, you, I, how many beers I owe you in the past. This one I'm going to pay off on. Okay?

CO-PILOT: Okay, we just cleared the runway.

GROUND CONTROL: Japan Air four six Echo heavy, taxi to parking. Say your gate number.

CO-PILOT: Roger, Romeo ten, and ah, it's very very extremely heavy turbulence, on ah, our take-off on [and] the left turn.

GROUND CONTROL: Roger, taxi to Romeo ten.

CAPTAIN: We ripped off some flaps and stuff.

ENGINEER: We did some damage . . .

CAPTAIN [looking out window at wing]:

Lots of parts missing out there.

ENGINEER: Good job guys, both of ya.

CAPTAIN: Thank you for your help. Sorry we got disorganized.

ENGINEER: Okay, should we do some of the others, after landing? I'm gonna to turn the probe heat and all that kind of stuff off, though.

CAPTAIN: Yeah, go ahead. I got the spoilers . . .

ENGINEER: That was cool, that fighter out there takin' our pictures.

CAPTAIN: Did we lose number two engine?

ENGINEER: Yes we did.

CO-PILOT: No . . . huh? Yeah, wait a minute.

ENGINEER: We lost it. We lost number two engine.

CAPTAIN: I had a hard time gettin' this thing trimmed enough . . .

ENGINEER: Jeez, that bank angle and stuff, man, that was like crazy.

CAPTAIN: I was goin' full full right rudder to recover the bank.

ENGINEER: I admit it now. I was scared.

CAPTAIN: We were all scared.

More than three minutes go by as they taxi to a stop at the terminal.

ENGINEER: Okay, somebody can kiss me and tell me I'm still here . . .

CAPTAIN: I'll kiss you in a minute here . . .

END OF TAPE

The No. 2 engine pylon had separated from the wing, taking the engine with it and damaging the wing slats and flaps. Load forces created by severe or possibly extreme turbulence caused the failure of the pylon, which was later tested and discovered to have contained a weakening metal-fatigue crack.

No one on board the airplane or on the ground was injured.

This was the fatal accident in the farmland of northern Indiana that made aviation authorities and the flying public seriously question commuter airline safety; it was the third crash involving a popular commuter airplane made by a French–Italian consortium.

All airplane accidents that result in fatalities are atrocious, of course, but this one seemed more so, if for no other reason than the way the victims were described by the coroner who examined them when he wrote that the passengers, all of whom died, had suffered 'multiple anatomical separations secondary to velocity impact of aircraft accident'. DNA had to be used to identify the bodies of the Captain and Co-pilot. Local authorities declared the crash site, which spread over 20 acres of a sodden soybean field, a 'biohazard area', with all that that term implies.

American Eagle Flight 4184, a twin-engined propeller-driven Avions de Transport Regional 72–212 (ATR 72), boarded late at Indianapolis Airport under threatening skies. Most of the flight's 64 passengers were returning home to Chicago after a day of doing business in the Indianapolis area, or they were planning to catch connecting flights out of Chicago–O'Hare. One passenger was worried about missing his connecting international flight to Frankfurt, Germany. Flight 4184 was due to leave Indianapolis at 2.10 p.m. (to arrive at O'Hare at 3.15 p.m.), but because of worsening weather at Chicago–O'Hare, the flight left the Indianapolis gate at 2.14 and was held on the ground for 42 minutes before taking off. At 2.53, the ground controller at Indianapolis advised the crew of Flight 4184 'to expect a little bit of holding in the air'.

At the time of the flight there was no particular warning about the icy conditions below 19,000 feet. The NTSB concluded that 'there were no additional reports of any significant weather phenomenon in the vicinity' of Flight 4184's holding pattern. But, as the flight circled in the holding pattern, little by little ice built up on the aileron assembly out of reach of the de-icing mechanisms. This ice would eventually reach a thickness that caused the airplane to roll over and plummet to the earth.

We pick up the CVR as Flight 4184 begins its turn into the holding pattern for Chicago–O'Hare.

COCKPIT: [Sound of music]

FLIGHT ATTENDANT: [I thought] I'd come to see what's going on up here.

COCKPIT: [Sound of loud music]

FLIGHT ATTENDANT: Is that like stereo, radio? You don't have a hard job at all. We're back there [in the passenger cabin] slugging it out with these people [passengers].

CAPTAIN: Yeah, you are. We do have it pretty easy. I was telling Jeff [Co-pilot], I don't think I'd ever want to do anything else but this.

CO-PILOT: [Agrees with the Captain's assessment] I, I like dealing [with] people in a way. It's kinda neat to be able to talk to them.

FLIGHT ATTENDANT: How late are we going to be?

CAPTAIN: Well . . .

FLIGHT ATTENDANT: We already got two people [passengers] that have already missed their [connecting] flights.

CAPTAIN: Oh, really?

FLIGHT ATTENDANT: Three fifteen [p.m.] is one of them. [Flight 4184 was originally scheduled to land at 3.10 p.m.]

CAPTAIN: Three fifteen, three fifteen?

FLIGHT ATTENDANT: [joking]: [And] it's all your fault. Uh huh. We weren't due in Chicago until three fifteen.

CAPTAIN: Three fifteen eastern time.

Passengers knew they might miss their connecting flights at Chicago–O'Hare before they left the ground at Indianapolis. The captain is probably making a joke or he was mistaken: 3.15 Eastern Standard time would have been 2.15 Chicago time.

FLIGHT ATTENDANT TO CREW: What do you do up here when [you are] autopiloting? Just hang out?

CO-PILOT: You still gotta tell it [the autopilot] what to do.

CAPTAIN: If the autopilot did not work, he'd [the Co-pilot who was flying the aircraft] be one busy little bee right now.

COCKPIT: [Sound of laughter]

FLIGHT ATTENDANT TO CAPTAIN: So, does

the [Co-pilot] do a lot more work than you do?

CAPTAIN: Yep.

COCKPIT: [Sound of laughter]

CO-PILOT: Not really.

CAPTAIN: Man, this thing [the airplane] gets a high deck angle in these turns [in the holding pattern].

CO-PILOT: Yeah.

CAPTAIN: We're just wallowing in the air just now.

CO-PILOT: You want flaps fifteen?

CAPTAIN [jokingly]: I'll be ready for that stall procedure here pretty soon [if the sluggishness of the airplane continues].

COCKPIT: [Laughter]

CAPTAIN: Do you want [to] kick 'em [the flaps] in? [It'll] bring the nose down.

CO-PILOT: Sure.

The Flight Attendant asks about the recorded warning voices in the cockpit. She thinks that they also warn about the presence of rain.

CAPTAIN: Rain?

CO-PILOT: No, this one maybe?

FLIGHT ATTENDANT: Sounds like it said something about the rain, or . . .

COCKPIT [the captain causes the alarm warning voices to sound for the flight attendant]: [Sound of warning: *Glideslope, whoop, whoop, pull up, whoop, whoop, pull up!*]

CAPTAIN: That one [you mean]?

FLIGHT ATTENDANT: Yeah, but there's something else.

CO-PILOT [joking with Flight Attendant]: Like I said, [if] it's a rain cloud, [recorded voices] say [it's rain]. Well, how do you know [there is rain]? Because this thing tells me. It'll [Ground Proximity Warning System] tell you: Ter*rain*, ter*rain*.

FLIGHT ATTENDANT: That's what it says? Ter*rain*?

The Captain or the Co-pilot then play the recorded voice for the Flight Attendant to hear.

COCKPIT: [Sound of warning: *Too low terrain, too low terrain*]

COCKPIT: [Sound of a local radio playing music]

COCKPIT: [Low frequency sound starts and increases as the revolutions per minute of the propellers automatically increases]

FLIGHT ATTENDANT: See you all.

CAPTAIN: All right.

COCKPIT: [Sound of cockpit door being opened and closed]

COCKPIT: [Low frequency sound decreases indicating a decrease in propeller rpms]

CO-PILOT TO CAPTAIN: Let's see. We got about, uh, thirty-six hundred pounds of fuel?

CAPTAIN: Uh huh.

COCKPIT: [Music stops]

CAPTAIN TO PASSENGERS ON INTERCOM: Well, folks, once again this is the Captain. [We] do regret to inform you that air-traffic control has put us into a holding pattern up here. We're holding for approximately twenty minutes out of Chicago at this time, but, uh, I guess the congestion and traffic's continued on, uh . . . They need us to hold out here for some spacing. They're saying at this point, uh, on the hour before we depart the hold, though that may not hold, uh . . . We may not be here the full thirteen minutes. We'll be sure to keep you updated. Once we leave the hold we'll let you know more if they tell us the hold is going to be a little bit longer. I do apologize for all these delays. Chances are that all the flights in and out of Chicago here this afternoon are going to be delayed as well. This is not just aircraft in the air just now but this is also, uh, for aircraft that were in the air earlier, aircraft on the ground and aircraft that are going to be departing. So, uh, once again, chances are that your connecting flight would be delayed also, and you'll still have a real good chance of making your connection. If not, they'll, uh, automatically re-book you on the next flight in Chicago.

The Captain and the Co-pilot discuss a bit of shared confusion about the workings of ACARS, which is a message system from the ground, usually the company offices, to the cockpit printed out on hard copy.

CO-PILOT: That's much nicer, flaps fifteen.

CAPTAIN: Yeah.

CO-PILOT: I'm showing some ice now.

The Captain needs to go to the bathroom badly.

CAPTAIN: I can't hold [it] any more, man. That big [thing?] needs out. Right now.

CO-PILOT: [Chuckles] They're gonna be giving you dirty looks [for going back through the cabin to the bathroom], man.

CAPTAIN: Oh, man, oh yeah. I know they are. People [passengers] do. It's either that or pee on 'em.

COCKPIT: [Sound of chime similar to flight attendant call bell; sound similar to seat belt being unfastened]

CAPTAIN TO FLIGHT ATTENDANT ON INTERPHONE: What's up?

FLIGHT ATTENDANT [calling the cockpit]: It's just me.

CAPTAIN: Huh?

FLIGHT ATTENDANT: I'm, uh. It was just me.

CAPTAIN: Oh.

FLIGHT ATTENDANT: I'm just wondering how much gas we got?

CAPTAIN: How much gas we got?

FLIGHT ATTENDANT: Yeah.

CAPTAIN: We got more than plenty of gas. We can be out here for a long time.

FLIGHT ATTENDANT: Cool. Okay. [I] just was worried [that] maybe you'd have to divert somewhere [for gas] and really make these people late.

CO-PILOT: Sixty miles from Chicago.

CAPTAIN: Oh, yeah.

FLIGHT ATTENDANT: Six, sixty miles?

CO-PILOT: Yeah.

FLIGHT ATTENDANT: Yeah, but they're still gonna hold us, huh?

CAPTAIN: 'Til about another ten minutes.

FLIGHT ATTENDANT: And that's not a for-sure thing, is it?

CAPTAIN: Yeah, pretty for-sure as of right now, unless they decide to make it different. How's that for an answer?

FLIGHT ATTENDANT: [Chuckles] Same like the other one.

CAPTAIN: Yeah, I know.

CAPTAIN TO CO-PILOT: Talk to her, bro.

Here the Captain gets up and goes back to the bathroom, leaving the Co-pilot alone at the controls.

CO-PILOT: Okay. Hey, you there?

FLIGHT ATTENDANT TO CO-PILOT: Are you sure you can handle it up there?

CO-PILOT: I'll try.

FLIGHT ATTENDANT: Okay, uh . . .

CO-PILOT: Why do you . . .

FLIGHT ATTENDANT: Turn it [the heat] down. It needs to be cooler back here. It's hot.

CO-PILOT: I'm, uh, it's all the way [turned] down now.

FLIGHT ATTENDANT: Okay, thanks. It's been down?

CO-PILOT: Yeah, well, I'll chill it up . . .

FLIGHT ATTENDANT: Really? Well, we're sweatin' [sound of panting].

CO-PILOT: You know why?

FLIGHT ATTENDANT: You want to hear us breathe heavy? [Sound of laughter]

CO-PILOT: It's one of the bleeds [that] are off.

FLIGHT ATTENDANT: Okay.

CO-PILOT: [One of the bleeds] for the air conditioning.

FLIGHT ATTENDANT: Yeah.

CO-PILOT: And it's [on] your side.

FLIGHT ATTENDANT: Oh.

CO-PILOT: It's the one that gives you [the] most of the air back there.

FLIGHT ATTENDANT: Figures.

CO-PILOT: So now you got, you got less than, uh, half, not only that. It's your half. [Sound of chuckle]

FLIGHT ATTENDANT: Okay. Okay, well here. Orlando [the Captain] wants to talk to you.

CO-PILOT: Orlando does? Hello.

CAPTAIN [on intercom from the back of the airplane]: Hey, bro.

CO-PILOT: Yeah.

CAPTAIN: [I'm] gettin' busy with the ladies back here.

CO-PILOT: Oh.

FLIGHT ATTENDANT: [Sound of snicker]

CAPTAIN: Yeah, so if, so if I don't make it up there within the next, say, fifteen or twenty minutes, you know why.

CO-PILOT: Okay. I'll, uh. When we get close to touchdown, I'll give you a ring.

CAPTAIN: There you go. No, I'll be up right now. There's somebody in the bathroom, so . . . Talk to you later.

CO-PILOT: Okay.

CAPTAIN [re-entering the cockpit]: We have a whole new hombre [after going to the bathroom]. Did you get any more messages from the cabbage patch [from the company on ACARS]?

CO-PILOT: No . . .

A minute goes by. The crew discusses where they put the paper with the list of connecting gates at O'Hare.

CAPTAIN: We still got ice.

COCKPIT: [Sound of paper being torn from the ACARS printer]

CAPTAIN: Here.

CO-PILOT: Got a message?

CAPTAIN: You did. I'll be right back. Okay, I'm [going] to talk to the company.

CENTER: Eagle Flight one eighty-four, descend and maintain eight thousand [feet].

CAPTAIN [calls the company offices at O'Hare]: Chicago, do you copy forty, one eighty-four?

COMPANY: Forty, one eighty-four. Go ahead.

CAPTAIN: Yeah, we've already been talking to dispatch, uh, on the ACARS, so they are aware of our delay. I don't know if you guys got the word on that. We're on a hold out here, uh . . . We got thirty-two hundred pounds [of fuel], thirty-three hundred pounds of fuel. They're saying zero zero . . . so in about another four or five minutes we'll find what the new word is. But what can you tell me about, um . . . There's this guy [passenger who is] concerned about his Frankfurt [Germany] connection. Uh, do you know anything about that?

CENTER: Eagle flight one eighty-four, descend and maintain eight thousand [feet].

CO-PILOT: Down to eight thousand, Eagle Flight one eighty-four.

CENTER: Eagle flight one eighty-four, uh, should be about ten minutes, uh, till you're cleared in.

COMPANY TO CAPTAIN: Uh, I can double check on that, uh, yeah. Just sent a message to dispatch to see if you were in a hold. Copy thirty on the fuel and estimated out time on the hour. And did you have that, uh, Frankfurt flight number, by any chance?

CO-PILOT TO CAPTAIN: They say ten more minutes [until cleared to land].

CAPTAIN TO COMPANY: Um, no. I sure don't, but I pulled up connecting gates out of the ACARS, and it says it's [the Frankfurt flight is] going out of [gate] K-Five, if that helps at all.

COMPANY: Let me check.

CAPTAIN TO CO-PILOT: Are we out of the hold [yet]?

CO-PILOT: Uh, no. We're just goin' to eight thousand.

CAPTAIN: Okay.

CO-PILOT: And, uh, ten more minutes, she [the controller] said.

COCKPIT: [Sound of beeps warning of overspeed]

CO-PILOT: Oops.

CAPTAIN: We . . . I knew we'd do that.

CO-PILOT: It's tryin' to keep it at one eighty [mph]. [A repetitive thudding sound]

COCKPIT: [A wailing sound warning of pitch trim movement]

It is at this point that, without any warning, the airplane flies out of control. The airplane rolled rapidly to the right. In a matter of seconds, the airplane was falling at 500 feet per second, pulling a G-force rating of 3.6.

CO-PILOT: Oops.

COCKPIT: [Sound of three thumps followed by rattling; sound of chirps consistent with the autopilot disconnecting; sound of altitude alert signal]

CREW: Okay. [Intermittent heavy irregular breathing starts and continues to end of recording]

CREW: Oh shit.

CAPTAIN: Okay.

COCKPIT: [Sound of altitude-alert horn]

CREW: [Sound of a growl continues for next twelve to thirteen seconds, until impact]

CAPTAIN: All right, man. Okay, mellow it out.

CO-PILOT: Okay.

CAPTAIN: Mellow it out.

CO-PILOT: Okay.

CAPTAIN: Nice and easy.

COCKPIT: [Terrain warning: *Whoop, whoop, terrain*]

CO-PILOT: Aw, shit.

COCKPIT: [Sound of loud crunching]

For the next 16 minutes, flight controllers at Chicago–O'Hare asked 17 times for Flight 4184 to respond.

END OF TAPE

All 64 passengers and the crew of four died instantly when Flight 4184 crashed nose-first in a wet soybean field 60 miles from Chicago. The NTSB concluded that the probable cause of the accident was 'the loss of control, attributed to a sudden and unexpected aileron hinge moment reversal that occurred after a ridge of ice accreted beyond the de-ice boots . . .' In short, ice interfered with the proper operation of the control surfaces. The autopilot held the airplane in level flight until it could hold it no more. Then switched off automatically, handing over the controls of an out-of-control airplane to the flight crew.

This incident typifies the adage that if it can go wrong it will, sometimes tragically, as in the case of Delta Flight 1141. While still on the ground at the gate at Dallas–Fort Worth International Airport, the Boeing 727–232 was serviced and prepared for a flight that would take it to Salt Lake City, Utah. The weather that afternoon, according to the Captain of the flight, was 'beautiful'.

Onboard were 98 passengers, three flight crew members, and four cabin attendants.

Before the engines were started, even before the Captain of the flight came aboard the airplane, a fueling agent checked the fuel in the No. 1 main fuel tank; then, according to habit, measured the airplane's pitch and roll (its overall balance) by the use of a plumb line in the aircraft's right main rear wheel well. These readings together were radioed to Delta Operations' senior customer service agent, who is responsible for the proper loading of fuel in the aircraft. The agent determined that the aircraft needed 1,036 gallons in the No. 1 tank for a total of 1,597 gallons.

An equal amount was ordered as a total for the No. 3 tank. The No. 2 tank was ordered to be filled to 10,600 pounds final weight.

The fueling agent went aboard the aircraft when he was finished to check the fuel gauges in the cockpit. The fuel gauge for No. 2 tank read 500 pounds higher than when he was on the ground fueling the aircraft. He mentioned this discrepancy to the Co-pilot.

The aircraft had landed in Dallas–Fort Worth with a No. 1 fuel quantity gauge in the cockpit that did not work. The Co-pilot knew about the gauge, as did the Delta mechanic who had handled the aircraft while it was on the ground. The gauge was not fixed but its status was noted in the aircraft's logbook.

While the flight was taxiing out for takeoff at 1.30 that afternoon, a lengthy delay inspired the Captain to shut down the No. 3 engine to conserve fuel. When the flight was number three in line for take-off, the engine was restarted. The delay lasted approximately 30 minutes.

Flight 1141 was already an accident about to happen.

We pick up the CVR as they are taxiing out for take-off.

GROUND CONTROL: Eleven forty-one, give me a right turn. Bring it between [the] south ramp and [taxiway] thirty. Hold short of inner [taxiway].

CO-PILOT: Eleven forty-one, roger.

Two minutes go by.

CAPTAIN [referring to the lack of attention given to them by Ground Control]: How about lookin' down here at Delta, now and then?

CO-PILOT: Yeah.

CABIN: [Sound of laughter]

FLIGHT ENGINEER: [Pay attention to us] while we're still young [referring to the delay]. How about lookin' down here while we still have teeth in our mouths?

CAPTAIN TO ENGINEER: What's that?

ENGINEER: [I said] how about lookin' down our way while we still have teeth in our mouths.

COCKPIT: [Laughter]

CO-PILOT: [We're] growing grey at the south ramp . . .

CAPTAIN: [The delay is] too long. I guess we ought to shut down number three [engine] to save a few thousand dollars [on fuel].

CO-PILOT: I'll, I'll call and ask Ground [Control] if we can . . . just, like, shut down over here. [I'll] ask him if he can give us a two-minute warning to start our engines.

ENGINEER: Okay.

GROUND CONTROL: Make a left turn and say your [flight] number.

CO-PILOT: That's eleven forty-one.

GROUND: Delta eleven forty-one, okay. Give way to company [another Delta jet] to your left, the [Boeing] seven-two-[7]. Join the inner for standard taxi [for take-off on] 18L.

CO-PILOT: Ah, seven-thirty, roger.

CAPTAIN: We're gonna wait for him [Delta's Boeing 727]?

CO-PILOT: Yeah.

CAPTAIN: Where is it [Delta Boeing 727]?

CO-PILOT: He's right there.

ENGINEER: He's comin' out.

CAPTAIN: [We] certainly taxied out before he did. Did he say standard to [Runway] Eighteen?

ENGINEER: Takeoff data has been computed for Eighteen L.

CO-PILOT: Okay.

For the next 15 seconds, the crew goes through the pre-take-off checklist.

FLIGHT ATTENDANT: A lotta people goin' out this morning.

ENGINEER: Yeah, [a] big blitz.

Now there are nearly eight minutes of conversation between the crew and the Flight Attendant.

CAPTAIN: Don't we have to change to ground here?

CO-PILOT: Yeah, I'm sorry. I'm sittin' here talking to the flight attendant.

The flight is given further taxiing instructions from Ground Control.

FLIGHT ATTENDANT: Are we going to take off or are we just gonna roll around the airport?

CO-PILOT: Well, we thought we were going to have to retire, sittin' here. They're

[Delta's Boeing 727] waiting for taxi clearance.

FLIGHT ATTENDANT: My gosh, we have got a long taxi to do.

CAPTAIN: Yeah, we're gettin' down here where we let all the Americans [American Airlines flights in line for take-off] get off first. Once they are all gone, we can go.

Another minute and a half go by.

CO-PILOT: What kind of birds are those?

ENGINEER: Egrets, or whatever they call them.

FLIGHT ATTENDANT: Yeah, egrets.

CO-PILOT: Are they?

FLIGHT ATTENDANT: I think so. Are they a cousin to the ones by the sea?

CAPTAIN: I don't know . . . Whenever I mow the grass out in my pasture they come in and it stirs up the grasshoppers and everything.

ENGINEER: Boy, they just flock here.

CO-PILOT: I've seen them all over the place out around here.

CAPTAIN: Grasshoppers . . . They [egrets] in fact, they sit on the back of our horse now and then. You see one out there just sittin' on the back of the horse.

FLIGHT ATTENDANT: Oh, is that right?

CO-PILOT: I've seen them sittin' on the back of a lot of cows.

CAPTAIN: Yeah.

FLIGHT ATTENDANT: Are they the ones that pick the bugs off of them and stuff?

CAPTAIN: I guess, and hang around them, because while they're [cows] are grazing, you know, they stir up the insects, and they [the egrets] can get them easier.

FLIGHT ATTENDANT: Uh huh. They're pretty birds.

CO-PILOT: They got one more American [Airlines flight in line] and I think we'll be able to go here. Start clearin' some of this . . .

CAPTAIN: It's interesting how they [the egrets] sit around the airport like this without being afraid.

SECOND FLIGHT ATTENDANT: Didn't we taxi [yet]?

CO-PILOT: I'm surprised they're [the egrets] not complainin' about the [jet] noise.

FLIGHT ATTENDANT TO SECOND FLIGHT ATTENDANT: We go to the other side [of the runway].

CAPTAIN TO FLIGHT ATTENDANT: All the way around down here, back up here.

ENGINEER: Boy, this [delay] is somethin'. If this is how it is on a severe clear VFR [a beautiful] day, can you imagine . . .

CO-PILOT: Imagine what it'd be like if we had weather today. I tell you what. Dallas–Fort Worth Center is a hundred per cent better than it was three years ago.

FLIGHT ATTENDANT: Is it really?

CO-PILOT: With regard to weather – gettin' in and getting out and all. If it clouded up and even looked like there was going to be weather . . . you'd be holdin', slowin' down, all kinds of stuff.

CAPTAIN: Did you see that bird?

FLIGHT ATTENDANT: Yeah.

CO-PILOT: He just got jet blast.

FLIGHT ATTENDANT: Yeah, he did. He got it.

CO-PILOT: Ah, what a crash.

FLIGHT ATTENDANT: [The egret must have said] what in the world was that?

CO-PILOT: [Did you] ever go out to Midway [Island in the South Pacific] and see the gooney birds? They're somethin' to watch.

ENGINEER: [The gooney birds] crash and look around to see if anybody saw 'em, you know . . .

CO-PILOT: Yeah. They would . . . If you would do a [engine] run-up, and the gooney birds would be back there in the prop[eller] wash just hangin' in the air, you know. And then they'd pull the power back [on the engines] and then [the gooney birds] would just . . .

COCKPIT: [Laughter]

CO-PILOT: . . . Hit the ground, you know. They were hilarious. They'd send a truck out. You'd get ready to take off. They'd send a pickup truck out and they'd go move the birds off the runway so you could take off.

FLIGHT ATTENDANT: Oh, really? Oh, how funny. Where are they? Where was that?

CO-PILOT: Midway, Midway Island. They come back and they nest in exactly the same spot [where] they were born.

FLIGHT ATTENDANT: On the runway?

CO-PILOT: Yeah, whether it was a runway or what[ever] it was. They come back to the exact same spot and, ah, so there's some kinda law or somethin' that you can't build anything on the island anymore because . . .

FLIGHT ATTENDANT: Uh huh . . .

CO-PILOT: [The island] it's a sanctuary for the birds or somethin'.

ENGINEER TO THE MAIN CABIN ON PUBLIC ADDRESS SYSTEM: Good morning, ladies and gentlemen. We're number four for departure. Flight Attendants, prepare the cabin, please.

FLIGHT ATTENDANT: We're ready [to go].

ENGINEER: Thank you.

COCKPIT: [Cockpit door is closed]

CAPTAIN: Might as well start [number three engine].

CO-PILOT: Number three.

ENGINEER: Start valve open.

CABIN: [Sound of engine starting]

30 seconds go by.

TOWER: Eleven forty-one, taxi position [to] Runway Eighteen L and hold . . .

ENGINEER: Shoulder harness.

CO-PILOT: They're on.

ENGINEER: Flaps.

CO-PILOT: Fifteen. Fifteen. Green light.

ENGINEER: Flight controls.

For the next 15 seconds, the crew goes through the pre-take-off checklist.

TOWER: Delta eleven forty-one, fly heading one-eight-five, Runway Eighteen L, cleared for take-off.

CO-PILOT: Eleven forty-one, one-one-eight-five, cleared for take-off.

The brakes are released, power is applied,

and the aircraft begins its take-off roll down the runway, picking up speed rapidly.

COCKPIT: [Sound of engines spooling up]
CO-PILOT: Power is set. Engine instruments look good. Airspeed is comin' up both sides. Eighty knots. Vee-R, Vee-Two.
COCKPIT: [Sound of snap; sound of the stick shaker]

Without warning, the aircraft rolled violently to the right.

CAPTAIN: Something's wrong! Oh . . .
COCKPIT: [Sound of engine stall]
CO-PILOT: Engine failure.
CAPTAIN: We got an engine failure. We're not gonna make it. Full power.
COCKPIT: [Sound of first impact; sound of second impact; sound of third impact]
COCKPIT: [Screams]
COCKPIT: [Sound of fourth impact]

END OF TAPE

The Captain later stated that 'all was normal' during the take-off roll, 6,017 feet down the runway at 177 mph. As the main gear wheels left the ground, the airplane began to roll violently, causing the right wing tip to contact the runway at 1,033 feet after lift-off. The airplane began to roll violently. 'It was all I could do to control the plane', the Captain said. He called for full power. He continued to raise the plane's nose. The Captain said, 'We're not going to make it.' There was a 'horrendous impact'. The aircraft struck an antenna array on the ground 1,000 feet beyond the end of the runway, and it came to rest 3,200 feet beyond the departure end of the runway. The airplane was destroyed by the impact and a post-crash fire. 14 people died.

The cause of the crash was later determined. The take-off 'configuration' was wrong for the aircraft. Its weight distribution, principally the fuel in tanks, caused the airplane to roll out of control the instant it left the ground.

The Challenger Space Shuttle was not a commercial airplane, nor even an airplane at all. But it did contain a black box which recorded the voices and sounds in the cockpit during the seconds before launch and the few seconds in-flight before the rocket destroyed itself over the Atlantic in a catastrophic failure of its booster-engine systems.

The commander of the shuttle that cool morning was Francis Richard Scobee, the pilot was Michael J. Smith and the mission specialists were Ellison S. Onizuka and Judith A. Resnik.

The tape runs for the period of T-2.05 (two minutes and five seconds) prior to launch, when the CVR automatically activated, through T+73 seconds after launch, until 'Loss of all data'.

Mission specialist Ronald E. McNair and payload specialists S. Christa McAuliffe and Gregory B. Jarvis, who were seated for launch in Challenger's middeck, were out of range of the cockpit voice recorder's microphones.

T-2.05 RESNICK [probably speaking to Commander Scobee]: Would you give that back to me? [It's my] security blanket. Hmm.

T-1.58 SCOBEE: Two minutes [to launch], downstairs; you got a watch running down there?

There were now two minutes to launch.

T-1.47 PILOT SMITH: Okay, there goes the LOX [liquid oxygen supply] arm.

T-1.46 SCOBEE: [There] goes the beanie cap [liquid oxygen vent cap].

T-1.44 ONIZUKA: Doesn't it go the other way?

T-1.42 COCKPIT: [Laughter]

T-1.39 SCOBEE: Now I see it. I see it.

T-1.39 SMITH: God, I hope not, Ellison [Onizuka].

T-1.38 SCOBEE: I couldn't see it [liquid oxygen supply arm] moving; it was behind the center screen.

T-1.33 RESNIK: Got your harnesses [seat restraints] locked?

T-1.29 SMITH: [joking]: What for?

T-1.28 SCOBEE: I won't lock mine; I might have to reach something.

T-1.24 SMITH: Ooh kaaaay.

T-1.04 ONIZUKA: Dick [Scobee]'s thinking of somebody there.

T-1.03 SCOBEE: Unhuh. One minute downstairs.

One minute to launch.

T-52 RESNIK: Cabin pressure is probably going to give us an alarm [a caution and warning alarm that was routine during pre-launch].

T-50 SCOBEE: Okay. Okay there.

T-43 SMITH: Alarm looks good [cabin pressure is acceptable].

T-42 SCOBEE: Okay.

T-40 SMITH: Ullage pressures are up. Right engine helium tank is just a little bit low.

T-32 SCOBEE: It was yesterday, too.

T-31 SMITH: Okay.

T-30 SCOBEE: Thirty seconds down there.

30 seconds to launch.

T-25 SMITH: Remember the red button when you make a roll call [reminder for communications].

T-23 SCOBEE: I won't do that; thanks a lot. Fifteen [seconds to launch].

T-6 SCOBEE: There they go guys.

Ignition of boosters.

RESNIK: All right.

SCOBEE: Three at a hundred [thrust level at 100% for all three engines].

T+O RESNIK: Aaall riiight.

T+1 SMITH: Here we go [vehicle motion].

T+7 SCOBEE: Houston, Challenger roll program [initiation of vehicle roll program].

T+11 SMITH: Go, you mother.

T+14 [Probably] RESNIK: LVLH [reminder for cockpit switch configuration change].

T+15 RESNIK: [Expletive] hot.

T+16 SCOBEE: Ooohh-kaaay.

T+19 SMITH: Looks like we've got a lotta wind here today.

T+20 SCOBEE: Yeah. It's a little hard to see out my window here.

T+28 SMITH: There's ten thousand feet and Mach point five [altitude and velocity report].

T+35 SCOBEE: Point nine [velocity report, 0.9 Mach].

T+40 SMITH: There's Mach one [velocity report, 1.0 Mach].

T+41 SCOBEE: Going through nineteen thousand [feet]. Okay, we're throttling down [normal thrust reduction].

T+57 SCOBEE: Throttling up [throttle up to 104% after maximum dynamic pressure].

T+58 SMITH: Throttle up.

T+59 SCOBEE: Roger.

T+60 SMITH: Feel that mother go. Woooohoooo. Thirty-five thousand [feet] going through one point five [altitude and velocity report, 35,000 feet, 1.5 Mach].

T+1.05 SCOBEE: Reading four eighty-six on mine [routine airspeed indicator check].

T+1.07 SMITH: Yep, that's what I've got, too.

T+1.10 SCOBEE: Roger, go at throttle up [boosters at 104%].

T+1.13 SMITH: Uh Oh.

T+1.13 LOSS OF ALL DATA.

END OF TAPE

The night of 20 December was starry over the Andes. Aboard Flight 965, an American Airlines Boeing 757 on a regularly scheduled passenger flight from Miami to Alfonso Bonilla Aragon International Airport in Cali, Colombia, there were 155 passengers flying home for the Christmas holidays, six cabin attendants and two cockpit crew members who were looking forward to a break in their schedule. The flight had left Miami late because of late-arriving connecting passengers and a one-hour and twenty-one-minute ground delay caused by airport traffic. But, after take-off, Flight 965 ascended to 37,000 feet over Cuban, Jamaican and into Colombian air space.

There was no evidence of a malfunction in the airplane. The weather was beautiful, but of course it was night over the Andes.

We start the CVR transcript with the flight a few minutes away from its initial descent into Cali over the caldera of the northern Andes. The aircraft was cruising at 37,000 feet with the center autopilot and both flight directors engaged. Heading was 189°. The Captain had apparently left the cockpit for the bathroom, and he returns, asking the Co-pilot what had happened in his absence, and they discuss the issues of crew layovers and scheduling.

CO-PILOT: Well, we did get the weather. It's good.

CAPTAIN: All right. She's [the Flight Attendant in the back where he had just come from] claiming they get an extra twenty minutes.

CO-PILOT: An extra twenty minutes, for what?

CAPTAIN: It's difficult [to explain] with the language problem, but . . . According to her figures, they're not legal to report to the airport until eight fifty. If we get in [land] at ten o'clock . . .

For the next several seconds, the Captain outlines the problems of his cabin crew; according to FAA regulations they must not fly more than a set number of hours without a rest, and those hours for this cabin crew are nearly up.

CO-PILOT: I got this little chart [that tells the FAA regulations about rest vs. flying].
CAPTAIN: Well, you see what you come up with. I'll watch the airplane and the radio. Okay?
CO-PILOT: Okay. All I see on this little chart they handed out is duty-on time, but it doesn't say anything about rest period.
CAPTAIN: That's another very confusing thing . . . I started to say, I wrote this little sheet out. I called [crew] tracking one day and I said, 'Hey, this fucking international [flying] is doing me, and I don't understand how a two-man crew . . . blah, blah, blah.' I said, 'I want you to spell out the legal rest,' and that's where I got this [little chart] from. And I wrote it down very explicitly. Ten hours minimum crew rest.
CO-PILOT: That's on international [flights]?
CAPTAIN: Yeah, if you fly less than five and a half hours.
CO-PILOT: Which is the case [here].
CAPTAIN: That's our scenario. Ten hours crew rest, thirty minutes debrief, and one hour sign in. And you can't move that up [change that] at all, because it's an FAA thing. You roll those wheels before eleven and a half hours, and you're fucked. Now, now, like I say. I can't, I'll have you know, grab a little extra half hour for us. We'll report a little bit late, just [to] give us a little extra sleep[ing] time. As long as we get the thing [the airplane] off at nine fifty [the next morning], so we don't get our asses [caught by the clock], [and they'll ask] why the hell didn't you report? To which I will say, 'The thirty- [or] forty-minute cab ride each way [from the airport to the hotel and] I don't think we had enough legal safe time. Now, if you want to hang me on that, you hang me on that, but I didn't break any FAA regulations. Anyway, you know . . . When you want descent, let me know a few minutes early in case there's a language problem [with the local controllers], okay?
CO-PILOT: Sure.
CAPTAIN: I can get through [to them linguistically].

Again, they beef about cockpit fatigue, mentioning a 'miserable last four hours' and 'these eight and a half hour deals'.

CAPTAIN: Yeah, a friend of mine – I played tennis with him, and, uh, he used to fly that

Sao Paulo [Brazil route] all of that time . . . You're fuckin' killin' yourself doin' that shit. [Do] you really need that extra couple hundred bucks a month, or whatever, when it comes to retirement? But anyway, to each his own. But he said he didn't mind it. He didn't mind driving back home at five o'clock in the morning. But to me, I'm like . . . it's torture.

CO-PILOT: Yeah.

CAPTAIN: Torture in the car trying to keep awake and stay alive. I discussed this with my wife. I said, 'Honey, I just don't want to do this, [and] I hope you don't feel like I'm [unintelligible words]'. She said, 'No way, forget it.' She said, 'You don't need to do that shit.' [Sound similar to a yawn] Yeah, [he, the pilot who didn't mind driving at five in the morning] just retired [from the airlines] a couple weeks ago.

CO-PILOT: Yeah, I knew this was his last month.

CAPTAIN: Yeah, he's a good man. I like him. We're good friends.

CO-PILOT: He got robbed at knife point in Rio, wasn't it?

CAPTAIN: That's right. He got stuck [by the knife] a little bit, actually, too.

CO-PILOT [Turning to the business of flying]: We'll let's see. We got a hundred and thirty-six miles to the VOR, and [we have] thirty-two thousand feet to lose, and slow down to boot, so we might as well get started [with our initial descent].

CAPTAIN: All right, sir. And if you'd keep the speed up in the descent, it would help us too, okay?

CO-PILOT: Okay.

CAPTAIN TO BOGOTA CONTROL: Bogota, American nine sixty-five, request descent.

BOGOTA: American nine sixty-five, descend and maintain flight level two four zero [24,000 feet], report reaching [that altitude].

CAPTAIN: Okay, we're leaving three seven zero [37,000 feet]. Descend and maintain two four zero, twenty-four [24,000 feet]. Thank you, ma'am. American nine sixty-five.

BOGOTA: That's correct.

CO-PILOT: Twenty-four [thousand feet] set.

CAPTAIN: Yes, sir. I'm goin' to call the company.

CO-PILOT: Okay.

CAPTAIN: American Airlines Operations at Cali, this is American nine sixty-five, do you read?

OPERATIONS: Go ahead, American nine six-five, this is Cali ops.

CAPTAIN: All right, Cali. We will be there in just about twenty-five minutes from now. Eh, and go ahead [and give us] the weather.

OPS: Okay, sir . . . The temperature is twenty . . . degrees. The altimeter is two nine point eight, conversion to two six point seven one.

CAPTAIN: Okay, understand the weather is good. Twenty-three degrees, to nine nine eight. Two six seven one. Is that correct?

OPS: That's correct.

CAPTAIN: Okay, are we parking at Gate Two tonight?

OPS: Gate Two and, uh, Runway Oh one.

CAPTAIN: Runway Oh one, and the weather is good, huh?

OPS: Okay, captain.

CAPTAIN: See you on the ground, nine six-five.

The Captain then repeats the information on weather, heading and wind, the runway and the gate number to the Co-pilot who is flying the airplane.

CO-PILOT: Okay.

CAPTAIN: All right, baby.

CO-PILOT: Sounds good.

CAPTAIN: All right. And I'm gonna put the headlights on early here because there's a lot of VFR [visual flight traffic in the area] and who knows what good deal. So the headlights just might help us a little bit [to let other aircraft see us]. And also, what was that position? Was [it] five? We're just about at it, aren't we?

CO-PILOT: Yeah. Forty-seven [miles] north of Rio Negro. Uh, of course we didn't go to Rio Negro.

CAPTAIN: Sorry?

CO-PILOT: [I was] talking about the, uh . . .

CAPTAIN: Yeah, it was Rio Negro plus forty-seven I think . . .

CO-PILOT: Rio Negro plus forty-seven.

CAPTAIN: What's, what [does the flight plan] show lat-long [for latitude and longitude]?

CO-PILOT [looks for flight plan]: Well, let me find it.

CAPTAIN: Just out of curiosity.

CO-PILOT: I had the flight plan.

CAPTAIN: All right, I wouldn't worry about it.

CO-PILOT: There we go [he finds the flight plan]. North uh, zero five one four six. Four, so zero five forty-one . . .

CAPTAIN: We're past it. Okay, we're past it. We press on, right?

CO-PILOT: Right.

CAPTAIN: I'm going to talk to the people [passengers].

CO-PILOT: Okay.

CAPTAIN: I'm off. [Now into PA system]: Uh, ladies and gentlemen, this is [the] captain. We have begun our descent for landing at Cali. It's a lovely evening as we had expected. We'll pass a shower or two on the way in but, uh, at the field right now it's, uh, good visibility, the temperature is two three, that's twenty-three degrees Celsius, and if you prefer Fahrenheit, that's seventy-two degrees on the Fahrenheit scale. The winds are ten miles an hour from the north-west. It's a very very pretty evening. I'd like to thank everyone for coming with us. Again, I apologize for being late tonight. These things do happen sometimes, very frustrating, but there wasn't very much we could do about it. Again, I appreciate your patience in the matter. Like to wish everyone a very very happy holiday, and a healthy and prosperous nineteen ninety-six. Thank you for coming with us. [Captain to Co-pilot] I'm back.

CO-PILOT: Uh, I may have to slow down if it gets too rough.

CAPTAIN: Sure.

Now they are descending through 25,700 feet to their assigned level of 24,000 feet.

CAPTAIN: You want any of these nuts?

CO-PILOT: No thank you.

CAPTAIN: You want me to call for the water or do you want to wait till we get on the ground, 'bout your water?

FIRST OFFICER: Oh, I'll get it on the ground. One to go.

CAPTAIN: Aye, aye. You got the engine heat off. Good. [Captain to Bogota Center]: American nine six five is [at] level two four zero [24,000 feet]. American nine six five is level two four zero.

BOGOTA CENTER: Standby two minutes for [a] lower [altitude].

CAPTAIN TO CO-PILOT: Pretty night, huh?

CO-PILOT: Yeah, it is lookin' nice out here. Let's see, what is the transition level here?

CAPTAIN: Oh yeah, it's a good check. Eighteen thousand?

CO-PILOT: One ninety [mph], eighteen thousand, yeah. Well if she [Bogota controller] doesn't let us down in a little while, she's goin' to put me in a jam here.

CAPTAIN TO BOGOTA CONTROL: And American nine six five, request lower [altitude].

BOGOTA CENTER: American nine six five, descend to flight level two zero zero [20,000 feet]. Report leaving two four zero.

CAPTAIN TO BOGOTA: We're leaving two four zero now and descending to two zero zero.

BOGOTA CENTER: Call Cali frequency one one niner decimal one. Buenos noches [Good night].

CAPTAIN TO BOGOTA: Please say the frequency again.

BOGOTA CENTER: One one niner decimal one.

CAPTAIN: One one niner decimal one. Feliz navidad, señorita [Merry Christmas, miss].

BOGOTA CENTER: Muchas gracias, lo mismos [Many thanks, and the same to you].

CAPTAIN: Gracias. Center, American nine six five, leaving flight level two four zero descending to two zero zero. Buenos tardes [Good night].

CO-PILOT: Nineteen one or . . .

CAPTAIN: That's Cali. Cali approach, American nine six five.

CALI APPROACH: American Niner six five, good evening. Go ahead.

CAPTAIN: Ah, buenos, señor, American nine six five leaving two three zero, descending to two zero zero. Go ahead sir.

CALI APPROACH: The uh, distance DME from Cali?

CAPTAIN: The DME is six three.

CALI APPROACH: Roger, is cleared to Cali VOR, uh, descend and maintain one five thousand feet [15,000], altimeter three zero zero two . . .

CO-PILOT: One five.

Now Flight 965 turns right from heading 189 to heading 198.

CALI APPROACH: No delay expect for approach. Report [when you reach], uh, Tulua VOR.

CAPTAIN: Thank you. I put direct Cali for you in there [a reference to the airplane's Flight Management System computer, called the FMS].

CO-PILOT: Okay. Thank you . . . Two fifty below ten here?

CAPTAIN: Yeah. [On Public Address system to cabin]: Uh, Flight Attendants, please prepare for landing, thank you. I sat 'em down and . . .

CALI APPROACH: Niner six five, Cali.

CAPTAIN: Niner six five, go ahead, please.

CALI APPROACH: Sir, the wind is calm. Are you able to approach Runway One niner [19]?

CAPTAIN TO CO-PILOT: Would you like to shoot the one nine [Runway 19] straight in?
CO-PILOT: Uh, yeah. We'll have to scramble to get down. We can do it.
CAPTAIN TO CALI APPROACH: Uh, yes, sir. We'll need a lower altitude right away though.
CALI APPROACH: Roger. American nine six five is cleared to VOR DME approach Runway One niner.
CAPTAIN TO CALI: [We are] cleared the VOR DME to One nine, Rozo one arrival. Will report the VOR, thank you sir.
CALI APPROACH: Report uh, Tulua VOR.
CAPTAIN: Report Tulua. I gotta give you to Tulua first of all. You, you wanna go right to Cali, er to Tulua?
CO-PILOT: Uh, I thought he said the Rozo-one arrival?
CAPTAIN: Yeah he did. We have time to pull that out . . . [He refers to his charts – sound of rustling pages] And, Tulua one . . . Rozo . . . There it is. Yeah, see that comes off Tulua.

Flight 965 is now passing 17,358 feet with speed brakes deployed full over the next 42 seconds. Airspeed decreases from 347 mph.

CAPTAIN TO CALI: Can American Airlines, uh, nine six five go direct to Rozo and then do the Rozo arrival, sir?
CALI APPROACH: Affirmative. Take the Rozo one and runway one niner, the wind is calm.
CAPTAIN: All right Rozo, the Rozo one to one nine, thank you, American nine six five.
CALI APPROACH: Thank you very much . . . Report Tulua and [unintelligible] twenty-one miles, ah, five thousand feet.
CAPTAIN: Okay, report Tulua twenty-one miles and five thousand feet, American Nine uh, six five.
CO-PILOT: Okay, so we're cleared down to five [thousand feet] now?
CAPTAIN: That's right, and . . . off Rozo . . . which I'll tune here. See what I get.
CO-PILOT: Yeah.
CAPTAIN: At twenty-one miles at five thousand's part of the approach. Okay?
CO-PILOT: Okay.

Now the Captain inputs data into the computer.

CALI APPROACH: American Niner six five, [what is your] distance now?

CAPTAIN: Uh huh, what did you want, sir?

CALI APPROACH: Distance DME.

CAPTAIN: Okay, the distance from, uh, Cali is, uh, thirty-eight [miles].

CO-PILOT: Uh, where are we? We goin' out to . . .

CAPTAIN: Let's go right to, uh, Tulua, first of all. Okay?

CO-PILOT: Yeah. Where [are] we headed?

CAPTAIN: I don't know . . . what's this . . . ? What happened here?

CO-PILOT: Manual.

CAPTAIN: Let's come to the right a little bit.

CO-PILOT: Yeah, he's wantin' to know where we're headed.

CAPTAIN: I'm goin' to give you direct Tulua.

CO-PILOT: Okay.

CAPTAIN: [Turn] right now. Okay, you got it?

CO-PILOT: Okay.

CAPTAIN: It's on your map. [Or it] should be.

CO-PILOT: Yeah, it's a left uh, left turn.

Flight 965 rolls from left turn to right turn as their altitude passes through 13,600 feet.

CAPTAIN: Yeah, I gotta identify that . . .

though I . . . Okay, I'm gettin' it. Seventeen seven. [It] just doesn't look right on mine. I don't know why.

CO-PILOT: Left turn, so you want a left turn back around?

Flight 965 rolls from right turn to left turn, then into right turn again.

CAPTAIN: Nawww . . . Hell no, let's press on to . . .

CO-PILOT: Press on to where though?

CAPTAIN: Tulua.

CO-PILOT: That's a right [turn].

CAPTAIN: Where [are] we goin'? Come to the right. Let's go to Cali . . . We got fucked up here, didn't we?

CO-PILOT: Yeah.

CAPTAIN: How did we get fucked up here? Come to the right, right now, come to the right, right now.

CO-PILOT: Yeah, we're, we're in a heading select to the right.

CAPTAIN: And American, uh, thirty-eight miles north of Cali, and you want us to go Tulua and then do the Rozo uh, to, uh, the runway, right? To Runway One nine?

CALI APPROACH: Niner six five, you can land, Runway One niner. You can use

Runway One niner. What is your altitude and the DME from Cali?

CAPTAIN: Okay, we're thirty-seven [miles] DME at ten thousand feet. [To co-pilot] You're okay. You're in good shape now. We're headin' . . .

CALI APPROACH: Report uh, five thousand and uh, final to one one, Runway One niner.

CAPTAIN: We're headin' the right direction, you wanna . . .

Flight 965 passes through 10,000 feet in mountainous terrain to 5,000 feet. Neither crew member made an attempt to stop the descent despite knowing that they had gone off the published approach course for landing at Cali and were in a valley surrounded by mountains. One minute from crashing, the Co-pilot, who recognizes the deviation in their course, attempts to turn back to the 'extended centerline' of the runway, which was Rozo.

CAPTAIN TO CO-PILOT: Come to the right, come, come right to Ca . . . Cali for now, okay?

CO-PILOT: Okay.

CAPTAIN: It's that fuckin' Tulua I'm not getting for some reason. See, I can't get [it]. Okay now, no, Tulua's [fucked] up.

CO-PILOT: Okay. Yeah. But I can put it in the box if you want it. I don't want Tulua. Let's just go to the extended centerline of uh . . .

CAPTAIN: Which is Rozo? Why don't you just go direct to Rozo then. All right?

CO-PILOT: Okay, let's . . .

CAPTAIN: I'm goin' to put that over you.

CO-PILOT: Get some altimeters, we're out of uh, ten [thousand feet] now.

CAPTAIN: All right.

CALI APPROACH: Niner six five, [report your] altitude?

CAPTAIN: Nine six five, nine thousand feet.

Now they pass through 8,600 feet.

CALI APPROACH: Roger, distance now?

CABIN: [*Terrain, terrain, whoop, whoop*]

Autopilot disengages. The flight crew adds full power and raises the nose of the aircraft; the speedbrakes which had been deployed are not retracted.

CAPTAIN: Oh shit . . . Pull up, baby.

CABIN: [Sound of aircraft stick shaker]

Flight 965 rolls out of right turn. A radar altitude alert sounds. Landing gear and flaps are up.

CO-PILOT: It's okay.
CAPTAIN: Pull up. Okay, easy does it, easy does it.
CABIN: [Sound of autopilot disconnect warning. Sound of aircraft stick shaker stops]
CO-PILOT: Nope.
CAPTAIN: Up, baby . . .
CABIN: [Sound of aircraft stick shaker starts and continues to impact]
CAPTAIN: More, more.
CO-PILOT: Okay.
CAPTAIN: Up, up, up.
CABIN: [*Whoop, whoop, pull up*]

END OF TAPE

Flight 965 first struck trees on the east side of a mountain named El Deluvio at 8,900 feet. The aircraft continued over the ridge and crashed into the summit on the west side of the mountain. The flight crew had gone off course and descended into a mountainous area at night. The Captain and the Co-pilot, it was determined, had committed a series 'of operational errors that led to the accident'. None of the errors when taken alone was egregious; however, when added together, they became fatal. The crew was hurried after it chose to land on Runway 19, rather than Runway 01, and necessary steps were performed improperly or not at all. They lost what is known as 'situational awareness'. They overlooked the fact of the terrain they were flying over, and finally and tragically, into.

Four passengers survived the crash with serious injuries.

ValuJet Flight No. 592. In the parlance of the controllers, the airline was 'Critter', because of the alligator painted on its tail. It was a cut rate airline, but there was nothing cut rate about its crew that spring afternoon as it pushed back and taxied out from a flight from Miami International Airport to Atlanta, Georgia. The day was bright, with thundershowers to the north. The flight departed at 1.44 p.m., a little late because of bad weather in Atlanta.

We start the CVR just as the cabin crew is preparing the passengers for pushback and departure.

FLIGHT ATTENDANT TO PASSENGERS ON PUBLIC ADDRESS SYSTEM: The cabin has been pressurized for your comfort. If oxygen is [needed] reach up, pull down on the mask until the tubing is fully extended. Place the mask over your nose and mouth, secure it with the elastic band and breathe normally. The oxygen bag may not appear to inflate. However, oxygen is flowing. For those of you traveling with small children, adjust your mask first and then assist the child. And passenger-seat cushions on this aircraft may be used as a flotation device and detailed instructions may be found on the safety information card. Smoking is not permitted at any time while on board this aircraft. Also keep in mind, due to possible interference with navigational or communications systems, the following electronic devices may not be used during take-off or landing: portable compact disk players, portable computers and cellular phones which should be in the off position and stowed. Now in preparation for take-off, please fasten your seatbelt, return your seat back and tray tables to the full upright and locked position. Your carry-on luggage must be stowed in the overhead compartments or underneath the seat in front of you. On behalf of all ValuJet employees, we'd like to thank you for selecting us today. We hope you enjoy your flight.

CO-PILOT TO CAPTAIN: [Coughs] Shoulder harness?

CAPTAIN: On.

CO-PILOT: Parking brakes.

CAPTAIN: Set.

CO-PILOT: Fuel quantity?

CAPTAIN: Twenty-two three [hundred pounds].

CO-PILOT: Twenty-two three. Pneumatic crossfeeds?

CAPTAIN: Open.

CO-PILOT: Anti-collision light?

CAPTAIN: On.

CO-PILOT: Air conditioning supply switches?

CAPTAIN: Off.

CO-PILOT: Fuel boost pumps?

CAPTAIN: On.

CO-PILOT: Ignition?

CAPTAIN: On.

CO-PILOT: Before start checklist complete.

FLIGHT ATTENDANT: Do you want me to tell them [passengers] information about [flight] connections?

CAPTAIN: You can tell them as we get closer.

CO-PILOT: Oil pressure and N one.

FLIGHT ATTENDANT: And ladies and gentlemen for those of you that are all concerned about your connections, captain Kubeck just informed me as soon as we get a little bit closer to Atlanta, we're able to relay . . . them [to you] . . . We'll give you more information as we get it. Thank you.

CAPTAIN: Okay, we'll be ready [to go] in about two minutes.

GROUND CONTROL: Okay, thanks.

CO-PILOT: Uuuuuh.

The crew starts the engines.

CAPTAIN: Single engine taxi, please.

CO-PILOT: Single engine . . . APU electric and air is set. Air conditioning, uh, supply on the right side is HP off. Air conditioning auto shutoff is [in] override. Ice protection number two is off. Right pneumatic crossfeed open. Number two fuel control level is off. [Coughs]

CAPTAIN: Before take-off check.

CO-PILOT: Performance data and bugs, for a hundred and five thousand, flaps five, Vee two [is at] one forty-six [mph].

CAPTAIN: One forty-six set and . . .

CO-PILOT: Trim?

CAPTAIN: And, uh, one point nine nine across.

CO-PILOT: Yeah.

The crew goes through its complete set of pre-take-off checks.

CAPTAIN: Okay, um, let's see. Where do we

go? Three twenty-two off Dolphin [Miami]. It's a vector to Dolphin . . . And I'll set three twenty-two.

CO-PILOT: [Coughs]

The crew discusses headings and weather.

CAPTAIN: Okay . . . it's my take-off, it's my abort, flaps are five, Vee one [takeoff] min[imum] is one thirty-six [mph]. Runway heading to five. If we lose [power] on takeoff, depending which runway we go on, we'll, uh, do a visual back down the runway. When we're about number three for take-off, we'll start number two [engine to save on fuel]. Questions? No questions?

CO-PILOT: No questions.

CAPTAIN: Is that an old Connie [Constellation] back there behind those buildings?

CO-PILOT: Ah, actually, it's one of those L-1011s.

CAPTAIN: Just behind this dirt pile here.

CO-PILOT: Okay, yeah.

CAPTAIN: [It] doesn't even have paint on it. Twin tails right there. About two o'clock. Hold short of Zulu. See it right there, off to the right?

CO-PILOT: Ah, I see a [Boeing] Seven forty-seven there.

CAPTAIN: He's real close to us, right behind us. The antenna's off to our right here by that building . . . it's kinda camouflaged.

CO-PILOT: Oh this, this twin tailed thing here?

CAPTAIN: Yeah.

CO-PILOT: Oh, that's a, uh, that's, uh . . .

CAPTAIN: A Connie [Constellation]?

CO-PILOT: A Connie one twenty-one.

CAPTAIN: Yeah.

CO-PILOT: Son of a gun.

CAPTAIN: You want to test out the PA and talk to the people. Um, you can ask if they hear or whatever you want. Understood whatever you use for words.

CO-PILOT: [Coughs] Ladies and gentlemen, from the cockpit, uh, we're on a hold right now for crossing traffic on the ground. Ah, and we only anticipate maybe a five or ten minute ground delay here but, uh, we are cleared to Atlanta just as soon as they can get us out through all the traffic here in Miami.

FLIGHT ATTENDANT [on the interphone from the cabin]: There's a women [standing] up. She wants to use the bathroom.

CAPTAIN: Yeah, [but tell her to] hurry.

CO-PILOT: Did you say warm it up?

CAPTAIN: No, a woman's using the restroom. [I said hurry it up].

CO-PILOT: Aah.

CAPTAIN: Engine re-start check list.

CO-PILOT: [Coughs] Left pneumatics closed, right pneumatic is open, right air conditioning supply switch off. APU air is on. Fuel pumps are on. Ignition's on. Before start check list complete.

CAPTAIN: Ignition is on.

CO-PILOT: Number two [engine].

CAPTAIN TO FLIGHT ATTENDANT ON INTERPHONE: Is the woman who was going to the bathroom] still up?

FLIGHT ATTENDANT: Yes, she's up.

CAPTAIN: Nobody else [gets] up from here on in.

CO-PILOT: Oil pressure.

CAPTAIN: Check.

COCKPIT: [Sound of increasing rpm]

CO-PILOT: Lights out.

The crew goes through the re-start checklist for engine No. 2.

CAPTAIN: If we have to go back, we'll back it up with the ILS. If we have to abort, you'll tell the Tower we're aborting.

CO-PILOT: Okay.

CAPTAIN: We're next up [for take-off].

CO-PILOT: Yeah. That's gotta be frustrating for those American [Airlines] guys. [They] have to wait for the company to give them their take-off data.

CAPTAIN: I'd kinda like to have that problem. [Sound of chuckle] Position and hold below the line.

CO-PILOT TO PASSENGERS: Ladies and gentlemen, we've been cleared to the runway for departure. Flight Attendants please be seated. [To Captain]: Anti-skid coming on?

CAPTAIN: Yep.

COCKPIT: [Sound similar to cockpit door being closed]

CO-PILOT: Cockpit door is locked, ignition on, APU is off, flight attendant signal is given, anti-skid is armed, and TA, transponder is TA RA, pneumatic crossfeeds are closed.

CAPTAIN: Okay.

CO-PILOT: Annunciator panel is checked, take-off briefing is complete. Flood and logo lights.

CAPTAIN: Okay. Lights are on.

COCKPIT: [Sound similar to engines increasing in rpm]

CAPTAIN: Bleeds are closed. Set take-off power.

CO-PILOT: Power is set. We have ninety-five [mph], ninety-four [knots of airspeed].

COCKPIT: [Sound of aircraft nose tire riding over bumps in runway].

CO-PILOT: [A] hundred knots.

CAPTAIN: Check.

CO-PILOT: Vee one.

CAPTAIN: Check.

CO-PILOT: Vee R[rotate]. Positive rate.

CAPTAIN: Gear up.

CO-PILOT: Vee two. Five [on flaps].

CAPTAIN: Flaps up.

CO-PILOT TO TOWER: Afternoon departure, Critter five ninety-two is out of five hundred [feet] going to five thousand [feet].

TOWER: Critter five ninety-two, departure. Good afternoon. Radar contact climb and maintain seven thousand [feet].

COCKPIT: Seven thousand, five nine two.

CAPTAIN: Slats retract.

CO-PILOT: Slats retract. Following the Boeing straight ahead of us in a turn.

CAPTAIN: Okay.

FLIGHT ATTENDANT ON PA SYSTEM: And, ladies and gentlemen, Captain Kubeck will turn off the fasten seat belt sign just as soon as she feels it's safe for you to get up and move about the cabin. Until that time, please remain comfortably seated with your seat belts securely fastened. We also suggest for your safety that seatbelts be fastened even after the sign has been turned off. Shortly, we will begin our in-flight service. We are pleased to offer you a variety of soft drinks, coffee and juices. Cocktails are available for three dollars. Beer and wine are available for two dollars. As always, correct change is greatly, greatly appreciated. For a complete listing of our complimentary beverages, they may be found on page five of our *Good Times* magazine. For now, we just ask that you sit back and relax and enjoy your flight to Atlanta, Georgia.

TOWER: Critter five ninety-two, turn left heading three six zero.

CO-PILOT: Three six zero, five ninety two.

CAPTAIN: Three six zero, climb power, climb check.

CO-PILOT: Power's set. Gear's up and checked, flaps up, lights out, spoilers [are] disarmed, the ignition is off, fuel pumps are set, air conditioning shutoff is override, hydraulic pumps off and low, flood and logo lights at ten, and altimeters at eighteen.

CAPTAIN: Thank you.

TOWER: Critter five ninety-two, turn left heading three three zero.

CAPTAIN: Three three zero, five nine two. Six [thousand feet] for seven.

CO-PILOT: Six for seven.

COCKPIT: [Tone similar to altitude alert signal]

TOWER: Critter five ninety-two, turn left heading three zero zero [and] join the Winco transition climb and maintain one six thousand [16,000 feet].

CO-PILOT: [Coughs]

CAPTAIN: Okay, let's turn on the radar . . .

CO-PILOT: [We've] got something out there [a weather condition] about eighty miles out.

CAPTAIN: Okay.

CO-PILOT: That must be that thunderstorm.

CAPTAIN: There's a break here like . . . I'd hate to be in this thing at a hundred and eight thousand and in through this weather.

CO-PILOT: Yeah. You don't want to hold them [the passengers in their seatbelts] for a while?

CAPTAIN: No, they're okay for right now.

CO-PILOT: Flight attendants, departure check please.

COCKPIT: [Sound of beep on public address/interphone channel]

CAPTAIN: What was that?

CO-PILOT: I don't know.

CAPTAIN: We got some electrical problem.

CO-PILOT: Yeah. That battery charger's kickin' in. Ooh, we gotta . . .

CAPTAIN: We're losing everything.

TOWER: Critter five nine two, contact Miami center on one-thirty-two-forty-five, so long.

CAPTAIN: We need, we need to go back to Miami.

COCKPIT: [Through the cockpit door, sounds of shouting from passenger cabin]

From a female voice in the cabin yelling through the door: Fire, fire, fire, fire!

From a male voice in cabin yelling through the cockpit door: We're on fire, we're on fire!

COCKPIT: [Sound similar to landing gear warning horn for three seconds]

TOWER: Critter five ninety-two contact Miami center, one-thirty-two-forty-five.

CAPTAIN: [We are returning] to Miami.

CO-PILOT TO TOWER: Uh, five-ninety-two needs immediate return to Miami.

TOWER: Critter five ninety-two, uh, roger, turn left heading two-seven-zero. Descend and maintain seven-thousand.

COCKPIT: [Sounds of shouting from passenger cabin subsides]

CO-PILOT: Two-seven-zero, seven-thousand, five ninety-two.

TOWER: What kind of problem are you havin'?

CAPTAIN: Fire!

CO-PILOT: Uh, smoke in the cockp[it] . . . smoke in the cabin.

TOWER: Roger.

CAPTAIN: What altitude?

CO-PILOT: Seven thousand [feet].

COCKPIT: [Sound similar to cockpit door opening; sound of six chimes similar to cabin service interphone]

FLIGHT ATTENDANT TO COCKPIT: Okay, we need oxygen. We can't get oxygen back here. Is there a way we could test them? [Sound of clearing her throat]

TOWER: Critter five ninety-two, when able to turn left heading two-five-zero. Descend and maintain five-thousand.

COCKPIT: [Sound of chimes similar to cabin service interphone; sounds of shouting from passenger cabin]

CO-PILOT: Two-five-zero seven-thousand.

FLIGHT ATTENDANT: [We're] completely on fire.

COCKPIT: [Sounds of shouting, screaming of passenger cabin subsides]

CO-PILOT: [We are] outta nine [thousand feet]

COCKPIT: [Sound similar to loud rushing air]

CO-PILOT: Critter five ninety-two, we need the, uh, closest airport available . . .

TOWER: Critter five ninety-two, they're [the emergency vehicles] going to be standing by for you. You can plan Runway One two to dolphin now.

There is now a one minute and 12 second interruption in CVR recording.

COCKPIT TO TOWER: [We] need radar vectors.

TOWER: Critter five ninety-two, turn left heading one four zero.

COCKPIT: One four zero.

COCKPIT: [Sound similar to loud rushing air]

TOWER: Critter five ninety-two, contact Miami approach on corrections no you . . . you just keep my frequency.

CVR: [Sound of repeating tones similar to recorder self-test signal starts and continues; sound of rushing air]

TOWER: Critter five ninety-two, you can, uh, turn left heading one zero zero and join the Runway One two localizer at Miami.

END OF TAPE

ValuJet Flight 592 crashed in the Everglades' swamp about 18 miles northwest of the Miami Airport, from which it had departed minutes before. A fire had erupted in the forward cargo hold in oxygen generators, classified as HAZMAT (Hazardous Material) and used in aircraft passenger service units. The heat of the fire was intense, estimated at nearly 3,000°F, and spread through the entire cabin.

Everyone on board – 105 passengers, two flight attendants, a crew of two – died either on impact or from fire-related injuries. The airplane plummeted from 10,000 feet nose down, reportedly because either the Captain or the Co-pilot was slumped against the control yoke.

What made the wreckage particularly grim, a swamp swallowed up the ValuJet DC-9 without a trace. The aircraft could not be found right away because the impact of the hull of a Douglas DC-9–32 against the ground left no scar on the terrain.

The crash of USAir Flight 427, a Boeing 737–300, stumped crash investigators for nearly three years before they were certain enough of their conclusions to make them a matter for the public record. For many months after the crash, what happened in the skies near Pittsburgh remained a total mystery. An airplane carrying 127 passengers and a crew of five (two pilots) simply and without warning rolled over and dove straight into the ground while on its initial approach to land.

The day was clear; the flight was on a visual approach. The time was around seven in the evening. The nearest other aircraft was 4.5 miles away with 1,500 feet of vertical separation. The crew was in a jovial, even festive, mood. The Captain yawned as the tape began. Landing that evening was a little bit like bringing a train into a station.

We begin the CVR about 19 minutes from the flight's meeting with disaster.

FLIGHT ATTENDANT TO THE COCKPIT CREW: They didn't give us connecting flight information or anything. Do you know what gate we're coming into?

CAPTAIN: Not yet.

FLIGHT ATTENDANT: Any idea?

CAPTAIN: No.

FLIGHT ATTENDANT: Do ya know what I'm thinkin' about? Pretzels.

CAPTAIN: Pretzels?

FLIGHT ATTENDANT: [Do] you guys need drinks here?

CAPTAIN: I could use a glass of somethin', whatever's open, water, uh, water – a juice?

CO-PILOT: I'll split a, yeah, a water, a juice, whatever's back there. I'll split one with [h]im.

FLIGHT ATTENDANT: Okey-dokey. Do you want me to make you my special fruity juice cocktail?

CAPTAIN: How fruity is it?

FLIGHT ATTENDANT: Why don't you just try it?

CO-PILOT: All right, I'll be a guinea pig.

COCKPIT: [Sound similar to cabin door closing as Flight Attendant leaves the cockpit to get the drinks]

Flight 427 is instructed to reduce its speed to 210 knots and maintain 10,000 feet altitude. A few seconds later, the flight is instructed to contact Pittsburgh Approach on frequency 121.25.

CAPTAIN: Two ten, he said?
CO-PILOT: Two ten? Oh, I heard two fifty . . .
CAPTAIN: I may have misunderstood him.

Pittsburgh Approach asks them to turn left heading 100.

COCKPIT: [Sound of cockpit door opening]
FLIGHT ATTENDANT: Here it is [the special fruity cocktail mixture]
CAPTAIN: All right.
CO-PILOT: All right. Thank you. Thank you.
FLIGHT ATTENDANT: I didn't taste 'em, so I don't know if they came out right.
CAPTAIN: That's good.
CO-PILOT: That *is* good.
FLIGHT ATTENDANT: It's good.
CO-PILOT: That is different. [It'd] be real good with some dark rum in it.
FLIGHT ATTENDANT: Yeah, right.
PITTSBURGH APPROACH: USAir Four twenty-seven, Pittsburgh Approach. Heading one six zero, vector ILS Runway Twenty-eight Right final approach course. Speed two one zero.
CO-PILOT: What kind of speed?
CAPTAIN TO APPROACH: We're comin' back to two ten [210 knots], and, uh, one sixty heading, down to ten [10,000 feet], USAir Four twenty-seven. [To Co-pilot] What runway did he say? [To the crew] It tastes like a . . .
CO-PILOT: Good.
CAPTAIN: There's [a] little grapefruit in it?
FLIGHT ATTENDANT: No.
CO-PILOT: Cranberry?
FLIGHT ATTENDANT: Yeah. You saw that from the color.
CAPTAIN: [What] else is in it?
CO-PILOT: Uh, Sprite?
FLIGHT ATTENDANT: Diet Sprite.
CO-PILOT: Huh.
FLIGHT ATTENDANT: And I guess you could do with Sprite. Probably be a little better if you do.
CAPTAIN: Yeah. There's more?
FLIGHT ATTENDANT: One more.
CO-PILOT: Ah.
FLIGHT ATTENDANT: You got it.
CO-PILOT: Huh?

FLIGHT ATTENDANT: Cranberry, orange, and Diet Sprite.

CO-PILOT: Really nice.

FLIGHT ATTENDANT: It's different . . .

CAPTAIN: I always mix cranberry and the grapefruit. I like that.

FLIGHT ATTENDANT: Okay, back to work.

CO-PILOT: Okay.

COCKPIT: [Sound similar to cockpit door opening and closing]

CO-PILOT: I suspect we're going to get the right side.

APPROACH: USAir four twenty-seven, descend and maintain six thousand.

CAPTAIN TO APPROACH: Cleared to six, USAir four twenty-seven.

CO-PILOT: Oh, my wife would like that [drink].

CAPTAIN: Cranberry, orange, and Sprite.

CO-PILOT: Yeah. I guess we ought to do a preliminary.

The crew now goes through their pre-landing checks. Approach requests a left turn heading 140, and to reduce their speed to 190 knots.

COCKPIT: [Sound similar to flap handle being moved; sound of single chime similar to seat belt chime]

CO-PILOT: Oops. I didn't kiss 'em [the passengers] goodbye. What was the temperature? [Do you] Remember?

CAPTAIN: Seventy-five.

CO-PILOT: Seventy-five?

FLIGHT ATTENDANT ON PUBLIC ADDRESS SYSTEM: Seatbelts and remain seated for the duration of the flight.

CO-PILOT TO PASSENGERS ON PA SYSTEM: Folks, from the flight deck, we should be on the ground in about ten more minutes. Uh, sunny skies, a little hazy. Temperature . . . temperature's, ah, seventy-five degrees. Wind's out of the west around ten miles per hour. [We] certainly 'ppreciate you choosing USAir for your travel needs this evening. Hope you enjoyed the flight. Hope you come back and travel with us again. This time we'd like to ask our Flight Attendants [to] please prepare the cabin for arrival. Ask you to check the security of your seatbelts. Thank you.

COCKPIT: [Seatbelt chime]

CAPTAIN TO APPROACH: Did you say [Runway] Twenty-eight Left for USAir four twenty-seven?

APPROACH: Uh, USAir four twenty-seven, it'll be Twenty-eight Right.

CAPTAIN: Twenty-eight Right, thank you. [To Co-pilot] Twenty-eight Right.

CO-PILOT: Right, Twenty-eight Right. That's what we planned on. Autobrakes on one for it.

Throughout, Pittsburgh Approach is issuing instructions to other aircraft in the area.

CAPTAIN: Seven [thousand] for six [thousand feet].

CO-PILOT: Seven for six.

CAPTAIN: Boy, they [Pittsburgh Approach] always slow you up so bad here.

CO-PILOT: That sun is gonna be just like it was takin' off in Cleveland yesterday, too. I'm just gonna close my eyes. [Sound of laughter] You holler when it looks like we're close. [Sound of laughter]

CAPTAIN: Okay.

APPROACH: USAir four twenty-seven, turn left heading one zero zero. Traffic will be one to two o'clock, six miles [away], [and it will be a] northbound Jetstream [which is] climbing out of thirty-three [3,300 feet] for five thousand [feet].

CAPTAIN TO APPROACH: We're looking for the traffic, turning to one zero zero, USAir four twenty-seven.

COCKPIT: [Sound in engines increasing rpms]

CO-PILOT: Oh, yeah. I see the Jetstream.

CAPTAIN: Sheez . . .

CO-PILOT: Zuh?

COCKPIT: [Sound of thump; sound like 'clickety-click'; again the thumping sound, but quieter than before]

CAPTAIN: Whoa . . . Hang on.

COCKPIT: [Sound of increasing rpms in engines; sound of clickety-click; sound of trim wheel turning at autopilot trim speed; sound similar to pilot grunting; sound of wailing horn similar to autopilot disconnect warning]

CAPTAIN: Hang on.

Flight 427 is now turning over on its back at 6,000 feet and heading for the ground at 300 miles an hour. It would take another 16 seconds before the aircraft hit the ground.

CO-PILOT: Oh, shit.

CAPTAIN: Hang on. What the hell is this?

COCKPIT: [Sound of stick shaker; sound of altitude alert]

COCKPIT: *Traffic. Traffic.* [Sound through the cabin door]

CAPTAIN: What the . . .

CO-PILOT: Oh . . .

CAPTAIN: Oh God, oh God . . .

APPROACH: USAir . . .

CAPTAIN TO APPROACH: Four twenty-seven, emergency!

CO-PILOT: [Sound of scream]

CAPTAIN: Pull . . .

CO-PILOT: Oh . . .

CAPTAIN: Pull . . . Pull . . .

CO-PILOT: God . . .

CAPTAIN: [Sound of screaming]

CO-PILOT: No . . .

END OF TAPE.

The airplane struck the ground near Aliquippa, Pennsylvania in a slight roll to the left at an 80° angle of descent, nearly perpendicular, going an estimated 299 mph. At the point of impact, the wreckage was buried eight feet deep in the earth. The aircraft hull disintegrated and there was an intense fire. At the time of impact, both engines were running symmetrically and powered with thrust. The thrust reversers were stowed. The flaps were at a 'Flap 1' setting, and spoilers and landing gear were retracted. These were all expected positions for an aircraft during its initial approach for landing.

All souls aboard died instantly.

The mystery of Flight 427 led to the longest and most intractable crash investigation in the history of the NTSB, which has not yet determined the cause of the accident at the time of writing, though it suspects that the trail of this tragic event was started by the wake vortex of another aircraft in the seconds before the accident began. That was followed by a large rudder movement in Flight 427, perhaps to compensate for the wake vortex, which then spun the aircraft out of control.

On a regularly scheduled flight from Hilo to Honolulu, Hawaii, Aloha Airlines' Flight 243 took off and climbed to a cruise altitude of 24,000 feet. It was at that flight level when the ceiling area of the forward passenger cabin suddenly burst open in an explosive decompression. The ceiling separated from the airplane, leaving the passengers from the cockpit door to the front of the wing exposed to the elements as though they were riding in a convertible car. Riding along in terror, they could do nothing as the aircraft dove to an altitude level (around 11,000 feet) where oxygen was not needed. There were two pilots aboard that early afternoon, an observer in the cockpit jumpseat, three flight attendants, and 89 passengers.

We pick up the CVR just as the ceiling rips off.

CABIN: [Sound of screams; sound of wind noise]

The CVR microphones in the cockpit could not pick up any crew conversation for the next five minutes. However, the CVR recorded the crew's transmissions with ground control through the crew's oxygen mask microphones.

CO-PILOT: Center, Aloha two forty-three. We're going down . . . Request lower [altitude]. Center, Aloha forty-three. Center, Aloha forty-three. Maui Approach, Aloha two forty-three. Maui Tower, Aloha two forty-three. Maui Tower, Aloha two forty-three. We're inbound for a landing. Maui Tower, Aloha two forty-three.

TOWER: [Flight] Callin' Tower, say again.

CO-PILOT: Maui Tower, Aloha two forty-three, we're inbound for landing. We're just, ah, west of Makena . . . just to the east of Makena, descending out of thirteen [13,000 feet], and we have rapid depr– we are unpressurized. Declaring an emergency . . .

TOWER: Aloha two forty-three, winds zero four zero at one five. Altimeter two niner niner niner. Just to verify again. You're breaking up. Your call sign is two forty-four? Is that correct. Or two forty-three?

Here the crew, having reached 11,000 feet, takes off its oxygen masks.

CO-PILOT: Two forty-three Aloha – forty-three.

TOWER: Two forty-two, the equipment is on the roll. Plan [to approach] straight in [on] Runway Two, and I'll keep you advised on any wind change.

CO-PILOT: Aloha two forty-three . . . [To Captain] Do you want me to call for anything else . . .

CAPTAIN: Nope.

TOWER: Is that Aloha two forty-four on the emergency?

CO-PILOT: Aloha two forty-three.

TOWER: Ah. two forty-six.

CO-PILOT: Aloha two forty-three.

TOWER: Aloha two forty-three, say your position.

CO-PILOT: We're just, ah, to the east of Makena [at a] point descending out of eleven thousand [11,000 feet]. Request clearance into Maui for landing. Request the [emergency] equipment.

TOWER: Okay, the equipment is on the field

. . . Is on the way. Squawk zero three four three. Aloha two forty-three, can you come up on [frequency] one one niner point five?

CO-PILOT: Two forty-three. Can you hear us on one nineteen five two, forty-three? Maui Tower, two forty-three. It looks like we've lost a door. We have a hole in this, ah, left side of the aircraft.

JUMPSEAT PASSENGER: I'm fine.

CO-PILOT TO CAPTAIN: Want the [landing] gear?

CAPTAIN: No.

CO-PILOT: Want the [landing] gear?

CAPTAIN: No.

CO-PILOT: Do you want it [the gear] down?

CAPTAIN: Flaps fifteen [for] landing.

CO-PILOT: Okay.

CAPTAIN: Here we go. We've picked up some of your airplane business right there. I think that they can hear you. They can't hear me. Ah, tell him, ah, we'll need assistance to evacuate this airplane.

CO-PILOT: Right.

CAPTAIN: We really can't communicate with the Flight Attendants, but we'll need trucks, and we'll need, ah, airstairs from Aloha.

CO-PILOT: All right. [To Tower] Maui Tower, two forty-three, can you hear me on Tower?

TOWER: Aloha two forty-three, I hear you loud and clear. Go ahead.

CO-PILOT: Ah, we're gonna need assistance. We cannot communicate with the flight attendants. Ah, we'll need assistance for the passengers when we land . . .

TOWER: Okay, I understand you're gonna need an ambulance. Is that correct?

CO-PILOT: Affirmative.

CAPTAIN TO CO-PILOT: It feels like manual reversion.

CO-PILOT: What?

CAPTAIN: Flight controls feel like manual reversion [like the autopilot has switched off].

CO-PILOT: Can we maintain altitude okay?

CAPTAIN: Ah . . .

CO-PILOT: Can we maintain altitude okay?

CAPTAIN: Let's try flying . . . let's try flying with the gear down here.

CO-PILOT: All right, you got it.

COCKPIT: [Sound of landing gear being lowered]

TOWER: Aloha two forty-three, can you give me your souls on board and your fuel on board?

CAPTAIN TO CO-PILOT: Do you have a passenger count for the Tower?

CO-PILOT TO TOWER: We, ah – eighty-five, eighty-six, plus five crew members.

TOWER: Okay. And, ah, just to verify. You broke up inititally. You do need an ambulance. Is that correct?

CO-PILOT: Affirmative.

TOWER: Roger. How many do you think are injured?

CO-PILOT: We have no idea. We cannot communicate with our Flight Attendant.

TOWER: Okay. We'll have an ambulance on the way.

CO-PILOT: There's a possibility that, ah, we won't have a nose gear.

CAPTAIN TO CO-PILOT: You tell 'em that we got such problems, but we are going to land anyway – even without the nose gear. But they should be aware of . . . we don't have a safe nose gear-down indication.

TOWER: Aloha two forty-three, wind zero five. The [emergency] equipment is in place.

CO-PILOT: Okay, be advised. We have no nose gear. We are landing without nose gear.

TOWER: Okay. If you need any other assistance, advise . . .

CO-PILOT: We'll need all the [emergency] equipment you've got. [To Captain] Is it easier to control with the flaps up?

CAPTAIN: Yeah. Put 'em at five. Can you

give me a Vee speed for a flaps-five landing?

The Co-pilot can't find the Vee speed.

CO-PILOT: Do you want the flaps down as we land?

CAPTAIN: Yeah, after we touch down.

CO-PILOT: Okay.

The Captain and Co-pilot discuss the speeds for landing.

TOWER: Aloha two forty-three, just for your information. The gear appears down. Gear appears down.

CO-PILOT TO CAPTAIN: Want me to go flaps forty . . . ?

CAPTAIN: No.

CO-PILOT: Okay.

COCKPIT: [Sound of touchdown on runway]

CO-PILOT: Thrust reverser.

CAPTAIN: Okay. Okay, shut it down.

CO-PILOT: Shut it down.

CAPTAIN: Now, left engine.

CO-PILOT: Flaps.

TOWER: Aloha, two forty-three, just shut her down where you are. Everything [is] fine. The gear did . . . The fire trucks are on the way . . .

CAPTAIN: Okay.

COCKPIT: [Sound of engines winding down]

CAPTAIN: Okay, start the call for the emergency evacuation.

END OF TAPE

The Boeing 737 of Aloha Flight 243 was manufactured in 1969 and had accumulated 35,496 flying hours and 89,680 take-off-landing cycles. The cause of the separation of the ceiling of the aircraft was attributed to static overstress separations. The airplane was old, and the cycles of pressurization and depressurization had weakened parts of the fuselage. One Flight Attendant was killed. All the passengers landed safely, though 65 of them were injured to varying degrees, mostly minor.

I have chosen to end the CVR collection with this tape because of what it says about the professionalism and sometimes heroism of airlines' crews.

United Airlines Flight 232, a DC-10, was on a regularly scheduled flight from Denver to Chicago carrying 296 passengers, eight Flight Attendants, and three crew in the cockpit including the Captain, Al Haynes, who was a 58-year-old veteran of commercial aviation.

While flying at a flight level of 37,000 feet at 3.16 p.m., about 200 miles west of Dubuque, Iowa, the DC-10 of Flight 232 experienced an explosive failure of its No. 2, or tail, engine. The separation of the engine, the fragmentation of its fan blades and other parts, and the explosive force of the fan rotor parts severed the aircraft's hydraulic lines which controlled the aircraft's wing flaps, elevators, ailerons and rudder. In other words, all steering mechanisms were lost. For the next 41 minutes, Haynes and his crew maneuvered the airplane with the throttles of the two remaining wing engines. Haynes turned the aircraft in large arcing spirals from 33,000 feet to land at Sioux City, Iowa. The most amazing thing about him, as the CVR demonstrates, is that he did not lose his sense of humor in the face of the emergency. He knew their predicament, and yet he rose above it, especially when a representative of United Airline's System Aircraft Maintenance in San Francisco refused to believe what the crew of Flight 232 was telling him; his insistence that all three hydraulic systems could not have been destroyed became a running joke for the flight crew in the ongoing emergency.

CAPTAIN HAYNES TO SIOUX CITY APPROACH: Ah, we're controlling the turns by power. I don't think we can turn right. I think we can only make left turns. We're starting a little bit of a left turn right now. Maybe we can only turn right. We can't turn left.
APPROACH: United two thirty-two heavy, ah, [I] understand you can only make right turns.

HAYNES: That's affirmative.

APPROACH: United two thirty-two heavy, roger. Your present track puts you about eight miles north of the airport, sir. And, ah, the only way we can get you around [Runway 31] is a slight left turn with differential power or if you go and jocket it over.

HAYNES: Roger. Okay, we're in a right turn now. It's about the only way we can go. We'll be able to make very slight turns on final, but right now just . . . we're gonna make right turns to whatever heading you want.

APPROACH: United two thirty-two heavy, roger. Ah, right turn, heading two five five.

HAYNES: Two five. [To Co-pilot] Now the goddamn elevator doesn't want to work. Rolling right.

FLIGHT ENGINEER TO UNITED AIRLINES SYSTEM AIRCRAFT MAINTENANCE SAM ON RADIO: This is United two thirty-two. We blew number two engine, and we've lost all hydraulics and we are only able to control, ah, level flight with the, ah, asymmetrical power settings. We have very little rudder or elevator.

CO-PILOT TO ENGINEER: Very little elevator. [It's] hard or sluggish. [To the captain] Ah,

Al, do you want me to slew this elevator. Feel [it].

HAYNES: Yeah, whatever you can [do].

APPROACH: United two thirty-two heavy, fly heading two four zero and say your souls on board.

CO-PILOT TO HAYNES: Ah, now the nose is coming up.

SAM TO AIRCRAFT: United two thirty-two, understand that you lost number two engine totally, sir?

CAPTAIN TO APPROACH: Say again.

APPROACH: Souls on board, United two thirty-two heavy.

HAYNES TO APPROACH: Gettin' that right now.

ENGINEER TO SAM: That's affirmative.

SAM: Your, ah, system one and system three – are they operating normally?

ENGINEER: Negative. All hydraulics are lost. All hydraulic systems are lost. The only thing we have is the . . . [and he itemizes the systems that are working].

APPROACH: United two thirty-two heavy, can you continue your turn to heading two four zero?

CO-PILOT TO APPROACH: I don't know. We'll try for it.

SAM: Okay, United two thirty-two,

understand you have normal power on one and three engines.

ENGINEER: That's affirmative.

CO-PILOT: [I] wonder about the outboard ailerons. If we put some flaps out, you think that would give us outboard?

ENGINEER: God, I hate to do anything.

HAYNES: Well, we're going to have to do something.

SAM: United two thirty-two, is all hydraulic quantity gone?

There is a growing sense of incredulity here on the part of the sam agent; losing all three hydraulic systems just isn't in the odds book, and he doubts the truth of what he is hearing.

ENGINEER: Yes, all hydraulic quantity is gone.

CO-PILOT TO HAYNES: Level off.

APPROACH: United two thirty-two heavy, souls on board and fuel remaining?

CO-PILOT: Souls on board and fuel remaining. We have thirty seven six [on fuel].

ENGINEER: We've got thirty-seven four on fuel.

APPROACH: Roger.

COCKPIT: [Sound of two knocks on cockpit door]

SAM: Okay, United two thirty-two, where you gonna set down?

HAYNES Unlock the door.

Earlier, the first Flight Attendant heard the engine explode while she was picking up trays and she sat down on the floor until things seemed normal again. After Captain Haynes made an announcement to the passengers that they had lost an engine, she stood up and reassured the passenger sitting in seat 23A who was clutching a baby and a woman in 23E who looked very frightened. Captain Haynes then called her on the interphone and asked her to come to the cockpit. Once there he told her the situation. She should prepare the cabin for evacuation. She did not ask any questions because as she said, 'The cockpit crew was working very hard.' She did not gather the Flight Attendants together because she did not want to alarm the passengers, and so she informed each of them individually. She told them to secure everything as quickly as possible. The trays were picked up.

The first Flight Attendant was aware of a United Pilot who was travelling in the first class cabin in civilian clothes. A passenger pointed out the window to show her the right horizontal stabilizer, which was visibly damaged. She returned to the cockpit and described what she had seen to Captain Haynes, who told her that the landing would be 'quick and dirty'.

Her hands were shaking as she was putting away meal trays, and she postponed announcing the plans for the evacuation until she was 'sure that I could stand there and do it in the manner that I am supposed to'. She read the quick preparation speech to the passengers over the PA system. She added that infants on the airplane should be placed on the floor. She briefed passengers in seats 9A, 9B and 9C on the operation of the exit door and asked two men to assist passengers at the bottom of the slide during the evacuation.

Now, back in the cockpit, the crew is struggling to get Flight 232 down safely.

HAYNES: What's SAM saying?
COCKPIT: [Sound of three knocks on door]
ENGINEER: We need some assistance right now. We can't . . . we're havin' a hard time controllin' it.
SAM: Okay, United two thirty-two.

HAYNES We don't have any controls.
CO-PILOT: You want to go forward on it, Al.
COCKPIT: [Sound of two knocks on door; sound of landing gear warning horn]
HAYNES Now go forward . . . Now, let it come back. Got to lead . . . got to lead it . . .
SAM: I'll try to help ya. I'll pull out your flight manual.

Here Captain Haynes turns to address a Captain riding in the cockpit jumpseat [referred to as Jumpseat Captain].

HAYNES TO JUMPSEAT CAPTAIN: See what you can see back there [in the cabin], will ya?
CO-PILOT TO JUMPSEAT CAPTAIN: Go back and look out [at] the wing . . . and see what we got . . .
JUMPSEAT CAPTAIN: Okay.
HAYNES [Pull] back on the sucker.
COCKPIT: [Cockpit door opens]
CO-PILOT: Don't pull the throttles off . . .

For the next few seconds the Co-pilot and Captain Haynes continue to maneuver with the throttles, while the Engineer discusses the problem with SAM by radio.

CO-PILOT: What's the hydraulic quantity?

ENGINEER: Down to zero.

CO-PILOT: On all of them?

ENGINEER: [On] all of them.

HAYNES: Quantity, quantity is gone?

ENGINEER: Yeah, all the quantity is gone. All pressure is [gone].

HAYNES TO ENGINEER: [Did] you get ahold of SAM?

ENGINEER: Yeah, I've talked to him.

HAYNES: What's he saying?

ENGINEER: He's not telling me anything.

HAYNES: We're not going to make the runway, fellas. We're gonna have to ditch this son of a bitch and hope for the best.

COCKPIT: [Sound of three knocks]

HAYNES: Unlock the damn door.

CO-PILOT: Unlock it.

HAYNES: We've lost . . . No hydraulics. We have no hydraulic fluid. That's part of our main problem.

UNITED AIRLINES CHICAGO HEADQUARTERS DISPATCH: United two thirty-two, do you want to put that thing on the ground right now, or do you want to come to Chicago?

ENGINEER: Okay, we're, ah, we don't know what we'll be able to do. We don't think we're even gonna be able to get on the runway right now. We have no control hardly at all . . .

JUMPSEAT CAPTAIN [Returning to cockpit]: Okay, both your inboard ailerons are sticking up. That's as far as I can tell. I don't know . . .

HAYNES: Well, that's because we're steering . . . we're turning maximum turn right now.

JUMPSEAT CAPTAIN: Tell me. Yell what you want and I'll help you.

HAYNES: Right throttle. Close one, put two up. What we need is elevator control. And I don't know how to get it.

JUMPSEAT CAPTAIN: Okay, ah . . .

ENGINEER TO CHICAGO HEADQUARTERS DISPATCH: Roger, we need any help we can get from SAM, as far as what to do with this. We don't have anything. We don't [know] what to do. We're having a hard time controlling it. We're descending. We're down to seventeen thousand feet. We have . . . ah hardly any control whatsoever.

HAYNES TO JUMPSEAT CAPTAIN: The only help you can get is the autopilot and I tried that, and it won't work

JUMPSEAT CAPTAIN: It won't work. Okay . . .

HAYNES: Go ahead and try it again. Pull back, pull back, pull back.

CHICAGO HEADQUARTERS DISPATCH: Okay,

copy that, two thirty-two. San Fran [is on the] line. Give 'em all the help you can. We'll get you expedited handling into Chicago [to] put you on the ground as soon as we can . . .

HAYNES: You want full aileron and full elevator. No, no, no no no not yet. Wait a minute. Wait 'til it levels off. Now go.

ENGINEER TO CHICAGO DISPATCH: Well, we can't make Chicago. We're gonna have to land somewhere out here, probably in a field.

HAYNES: How're they doin' on the evacuation [preparations]?

JUMPSEAT CAPTAIN: They're puttin' things away, but they're not in any big hurry.

SAM: United two thirty-two, we [understand that you] have to land [at] the nearest airport, the nearest airport. Ah, I'm tryin' to find out where you've lost all three hydraulic systems.

HAYNES: Well, they better hurry. We're gonna have to ditch, I think.

JUMPSEAT CAPTAIN: Yeah.

HAYNES: Okay.

COCKPIT: [Sound of knock on door]

HAYNES: I don't think we're going to make the airport.

CO-PILOT: No. We got no hydraulics at all.

COCKPIT: [Sound of landing gear warning horn]

JUMPSEAT CAPTAIN: Get this thing down. We're in trouble . . .

ENGINEER TO SAM: That is affirmative. We have lost all three hydraulic systems. We have no quantity and no pressure on any hydraulic system . . .

HAYNES TO SIOUX CITY APPROACH: Sir, we have no hydraulic fluid, which means we have no elevator control, almost none, and very little aileron control. I have serious doubts about making the airport. Have you got someplace near there, ah, that we might be able to ditch? Unless we get control of this airplane we're gonna put it down wherever it happens to be.

SAM: Ah, United two thirty-two, you have lost all manual flight control systems?

ENGINEER: That's apparently true.

SAM: United two thirty-two, ah, in the flight manual [on page] sixty- . . .

HAYNES: Gotta put some flaps and see if that'll help . . .

ENGINEER TO SAM: I am on [page] sixty-three.

CO-PILOT: You want them [the flaps] now?

HAYNES: What the hell. Let's do it. We can't get any worse than we are . . .

CO-PILOT: Slats are out?

JUMPSEAT CAPTAIN: No, you don't have any slats.

HAYNES: We don't have any hydraulics, so we're not going to get anything.

SIOUX CITY APPROACH: United two thirty-two heavy, can you hold that present heading, sir?

HAYNES: This is Sioux City, Iowa. That's where we're headed.

There is confusion about where they are and how far they are from Sioux City.

HAYNES TO SIOUX CITY APPROACH: Where's the airport now for [United] two thirty [-two]? We're turning around in circles.

JUMPSEAT CAPTAIN PROBABLY TO CO-PILOT: You get on number one and ask them where the hell we are.

HAYNES TO SIOUX CITY: Where's the airport to us now, as we come spinning down here?

SIOUX CITY APPROACH: United two thirty-two heavy, Sioux City airport is about twelve o'clock and three six [36] miles.

HAYNES: Okay. We're tryin' to go straight. We're not havin' much luck.

JUMPSEAT CAPTAIN: All right, I got you on

seven hundred on the squawk, so they can track ya [on radar].

CO-PILOT: He's got us on radar.

HAYNES: As soon as the nose starts up we have to push forward on the yoke.

JUMPSEAT CAPTAIN: We got nothing on number two, number two [engine]?

HAYNES: No, no, we got it shut down.

SAM: United two thirty-two, I'm gettin' contact with flight ops right now. Standby please.

HAYNES: I want a heading of about three zero zero. We kinda got level flight back again.

JUMPSEAT CAPTAIN: Okay, if you got denser air, you should [get level flight back again]. Whatever you got you got.

HAYNES: A little better.

JUMPSEAT CAPTAIN: Okay, ah, let me see . . .

HAYNES: [Laughs] We didn't do this thing on my last [performance check in a simulator].

COCKPIT: [Laughter]

CO-PILOT: No.

HAYNES: [I] poured coffee all over . . . it's just coffee. We'll get this thing on the ground. Don't worry about it.

CO-PILOT: It seems controllable, doesn't it, Al?

JUMPSEAT CAPTAIN: Yeah. The lower you get the more dense that air is [and] the better your shots. Okay?

HAYNES: I'll tell ya what we need. We're puttin' this thing into Sioux City. Get me . . . [To Sioux City Approach] Sioux City, United two thirty-two, could you give us please your ILS frequency, the heading, and the length of the runway?

SIOUX CITY APPROACH: United two thirty-two heavy, affirmative. The localizer frequency is one zero nine point three and you're currently about thirty-five miles to the north-east. It'll take about [heading] two two two three five two four zero heading to join it.

SAM: United two thirty-two, this is SAM.

COCKPIT: [Sound of landing gear warning horn]

ENGINEER TO SAM: SAM, two thirty-two. We're gonna try and put into Sioux City.

UNITED AIRLINES HEADQUARTERS CHICAGO DISPATCH: SAM, this is dispatch. I haven't been able to copy two thirty-two. We're hearing a rumor that he's on approach to Sioux City airport. Last we heard he's at seventeen thousand feet and he may be too low for us to maintain contact with him. Go ahead . . .

SIOUX CITY APPROACH: United two thirty-two, understand you are gonna try to make it into Sioux City. There's no airport out that way that can accommodate you, sir.

HAYNES: Okay, we'll head for Sioux City. We got a little bit of control back now. How long [is] your runway?

ENGINEER TO SAM: Two thirty-two is very busy right now. We're tryin' to go into Sioux City. We'll call you as soon as I can . . .

SIOUX CITY APPROACH: Two thirty-two heavy, the airport, the runway is nine thousand feet long . . .

SAM: He has no control. He's using that kind of sink rate, I believe. This is what he's doing. He's got his hands full for sure.

HAYNES TO SIOUX CITY APPROACH: Okay, thank you. [To Jumpseat Captain] You're a little more . . . Let's see if you can make a left turn.

JUMPSEAT CAPTAIN: Left turn. All right. Your speed is what? I'm worried about [it]. I don't want to stall you.

CHICAGO HEADQUARTERS DISPATCH TO SAM: Okay, we just wanted [flight two thirty-two] to say where he was so we can get emergency equipment out. Thanks a lot, SAM.

ENGINEER TO HAYNES: You want a no flap-no slat [landing], right?

HAYNES: Yeah. Ah, start dumpin' [fuel] will ya? Just hit the quick [fuel] dump. Let's get the weight down as low as [we] can . . .

ENGINEER: I didn't have time to think about that [dumping fuel].

HAYNES: Try not to lose any more [altitude] than we have to.

CO-PILOT: What? Altitude?

HAYNES: Yeah.

CO-PILOT: Okay. Go ahead and dump.

JUMPSEAT CAPTAIN: He's got his weight. He's got his weight. He's only got about a thousand pounds [of fuel] to go.

CO-PILOT: Okay.

JUMPSEAT CAPTAIN: This thing seems to want to go right more than it wants to go left, doesn't it?

SIOUX CITY APPROACH: United two thirty-two, did you get the souls on board count?

CAPTAIN TO CREW: What did you have for a count for people? [to Sioux City]: [Let me] tell you, right now we don't even have time to call the gal [the flight attendants in the passenger cabin for a passenger count] . . .

ENGINEER: Ah, two ninety-two.

SIOUX CITY APPROACH: Roger.

HAYNES: Ease all the power back.

JUMPSEAT CAPTAIN: Okay, [the] nose is coming up.

SAM: All hydraulic systems are gone . . .

SIOUX CITY APPROACH: Okay, thank you.

CO-PILOT: Yeah, we're goin' up.

HAYNES Yeah, I know it. I'm pushin' with all I got.

JUMPSEAT CAPTAIN: [The] power's coming back. Power's coming back . . .

HAYNES: As soon as it starts to come back . . . Okay, come back . . .

JUMPSEAT CAPTAIN: Power's comin' back in . . .

HAYNES: Bring [turn] it to the right with the right one. You got to go left. We just keep turnin' right. Still turnin' right . . .

JUMPSEAT CAPTAIN: That's what I'm tryin' to do . . .

HAYNES TO SIOUX CITY APPROACH: Two thirty-two, we're just gonna have to keep turnin' right. There's not much we can do about [turning] left. We'll try to come back around to the heading . . .

CO-PILOT: Is this Sioux City down to the right?

HAYNES: That's Sioux City.

SIOUX CITY APPROACH: United two thirty-two, roger. [We] need you on about a two-three-five heading, sir, if you can manage that and hold that.

HAYNES TO SIOUX CITY APPROACH: Well, we'll see what happens . . .

JUMPSEAT CAPTAIN: [We're] goin' down now. I'll put a little bit more power [on]. I'm gonna try and set about ninety per cent [and] see if that holds up good for you. Tryin' to find the right power setting so you don't have to fight this pitch.

CO-PILOT: Ease it to the right.

HAYNES: Did you ever get hold of SAM?

ENGINEER: Yep. Didn't get any help.

HAYNES: [Sound of laughter] Okay, did you tell 'em to advise dispatch of our situation and what we're doing?

ENGINEER: Yes, he knows.

HAYNES: No more right turns, no more. Ah, I mean, ah, we want to turn right. He [Sioux City] wants us to turn right.

JUMPSEAT CAPTAIN: You do want to turn . . . all right?

HAYNES: [Sound of exhalation]

CO-PILOT TO SIOUX CITY APPROACH: Where is Sioux City from our present position, United two thirty-two?

SIOUX CITY APPROACH: United two thirty-two, it's about twenty [degrees] on the heading and thirty-seven miles . . .

CO-PILOT: [There is an] airport right below us here, but . . .

HAYNES: They said it won't accommodate us.

CO-PILOT: Okay.

HAYNES: See if you can keep us with the throttles in a ten to fifteen degree turn . . .

JUMPSEAT CAPTAIN: All right. I'll play 'em [throttles]. I'll play 'em. I'll power up this number three engine and try to accommodate you.

HAYNES: You had the thing leveled off for a minute.

A training Pilot for United who had been riding in first class, named Denny Fitch, comes into the cockpit to see whether he can assist the crew. The Jumpseat Captain gives him his place and he goes back into the cabin and takes a seat in the rear of the airplane.

HAYNES TO DENNY FITCH: My name's Al Haynes.

JUMPSEAT FITCH: Hi, Al. Denny Fitch.

HAYNES: How do you do, Denny?

JUMPSEAT FITCH: I'll tell you what. We'll have a beer when this is all done.

HAYNES: Well, I don't drink, but I'll sure as hell have one. Little right turns, little right turns.

Haynes and his crew discuss power settings and headings for a few seconds.

JUMPSEAT FITCH: You lost the engine, huh?

HAYNES: Yeah, well, yeah. It blew. We couldn't do anything about it. We shut it down.

JUMPSEAT FITCH: Yeah.

ENGINEER TO SAM: Go ahead with any help you can give us.

SAM: United two thirty-two, understand that you have [the numbers] one and three engines operating. You have absolutely no hydraulic power. You have no control over the aircraft. Is that correct?

HAYNES TO JUMPSEAT FITCH: [I] can't think of anything that we [haven't] done . . . There really isn't a procedure for this.

JUMPSEAT FITCH: No, the only thing I can think about that might help you at some point here [is to put] the [landing] gear down and that might hold the nose down a bit.

SAM: Okay, United two thirty-two, I've got operational engineering on its way over here, and at the present time you are doing just about everything that you can possibly do. Your flaps and slats, I believe, are in the up position, are they not?

SIOUX CITY APPROACH: When you get turned to that two-forty heading, sir, the airport will be about twelve o'clock and thirty-eight miles.

CO-PILOT: Okay, we're tryin' to control it just by power alone now. We have no hydraulics at all, so we're doing our best here.

SIOUX CITY APPROACH: Roger, and we've notified the [emergency] equipment out in that area, sir. The equipment is standing by.

ENGINEER TO SAM: That is affirmative. That is affirmative. That is affirmative. Do you read?

Captain Haynes confirms certain frequencies and headings for the final approach.

HAYNES: Everybody ready?

JUMPSEAT FITCH: Anything above about two ten [knots] is going to give you a nose-up moment . . .

HAYNES: We have almost no control of the airplane.

SAM: United two thirty-two, in your handbook on page I ninety-one, I ninety-one . . .

CO-PILOT: We have no hydraulics at all.

HAYNES: It's gonna be tough, gonna be rough . . .

FLIGHT ATTENDANT: So we're gonna evacuate?

HAYNES: Yeah. Well, we're gonna have the gear down.

FLIGHT ATTENDANT: Yeah.

HAYNES: And if we can keep the airplane on the ground and stop standing up, give us a second or two before you evacuate.

ENGINEER TO SAM: We already have a no flap-no slat [approach] made up and we're gettin' ready. We're gonna try to put into Sioux City with gear down.

CO-PILOT: Okay . . . pull back a little more.

HAYNES TO FLIGHT ATTENDANT: 'Brace' will be the signal; it'll be over the PA system – 'Brace, brace, brace.'

SAM: United, you're tryin' to go into Sioux City. We'll contact Sioux City and have emergency equipment available.

FLIGHT ATTENDANT TO HAYNES: And that will be to evacuate?

HAYNES: No, that'll be to brace for landing.

FLIGHT ATTENDANT: Un huh.

HAYNES: And then if you have to evacuate you'll get the command signal to evacuate, but I really have my doubts you'll see us standing up, honey. Good luck, sweetheart.

FLIGHT ATTENDANT: Thank you too.

ENGINEER TO SAM: Okay, we will be tryin' to get in there [Sioux City].

SAM: Okay, United two thirty-two, I'll stay with you.

ENGINEER: Okay, we will be waitin' in case you have anything more.

SAM: We're scurrying around and I've got people out looking for more information.

HAYNES: The heading is two forty.

JUMPSEAT FITCH: Okay, I'm gonna try to hold you about two ten. I'll just see if it makes a difference if I bump it . . . bump it up in the air. This may be the world's greatest tricycle . . .

ENGINEER [to crew after talking to flight attendant over interphone]: She says there appears to be some damage on that one wing. Do you want me to go back and take a look?

JUMPSEAT FITCH: No, we don't have time.

HAYNES: Okay, go ahead. Go ahead and see what you can see, not that it'll do any good.

[To Jumpseat]: I wish we had a little better control of the elevator. They told us the autopilot would do this, but it sure as hell won't. Try yours again.

CO-PILOT: Can't get it on.

HAYNES: Well, we've got the ah . . . ah.

JUMPSEAT FITCH: All right, we came into the clear.

HAYNES: Turn, baby.

JUMPSEAT FITCH: Which way do you want it, Al?

HAYNES: Left.

CO-PILOT: Left.

HAYNES: Come on back, come on back, come on back . . . As soon as that [is] vertical go for it, go for it. Watch that vertical speed the second it starts to move. Come back, come back, come back. Go for it. If we can get this under control elevator-wise we can work on steering later.

COCKPIT: [Sound of laughter]

JUMPSEAT FITCH: We need to go left again to get ready to go . . .

HAYNES: You keep goin' right two forty 'cause we still got two thousand feet to go. [To Sioux City] United two thirty-two, we're gonna have to continue one more right turn. We got the elevators pretty much under control within three or four hundred feet but we still can't do much with the steering.

SIOUX CITY APPROACH: United two thirty-two heavy, roger. Understand you [have] the elevators possibly under control [enough to hold] altitude?

CO-PILOT: Barely.

HAYNES TO SIOUX CITY APPROACH: Negative. We don't have it, but we are better, that's all.

SIOUX CITY APPROACH: Roger.

JUMPSEAT FITCH TO HAYNES: You want to turn right?

HAYNES: Yeah, let's turn right.

JUMPSEAT FITCH: All right, here we go.

HAYNES TO SIOUX CITY APPROACH: How far is the field now, please?

SIOUX CITY APPROACH: United two thirty-two heavy, you're currently thirty-three miles north-east.

COCKPIT: [Sound of three knocks on door]

HAYNES: Thank you. [To Jumpseat] Just let her ease down. I wish they'd unlock that damn door [or] pull the circuit breaker on that door. Just unlock it, will ya?

ENGINEER: Okay.

SIOUX CITY APPROACH: United two thirty-two heavy, there are a couple of really small airports out in the vicinity here, and Storm Lake is four thousand two hundred feet by seventy-five [feet]. That's about fifteen miles east of your position.

ENGINEER [who comes back into the cockpit after his inspection of the back of the airplane]: All right, I walked to the back and we got a lot of damage to the tail section. We could see through the window.

CO-PILOT TO SIOUX CITY APPROACH: Roger, we're still goin' down [and] tryin' to control it. As we get down a little lower here we'll pick it out.

SAM: Okay, United two thirty-two, you have a lot of damage to the tail section?

ENGINEER: The leading edge of the elevator is damaged. I mean, there's damage there that I can see. I don't know how much [there] is that I cannot see. I can see it on the leading edge, on the outer parts.

SAM: United two thirty-two, Engineering is assembling right now, and they're listening to us.

Captain Haynes announces his orders to the passengers about the warning to 'brace'.

ENGINEER TO SAM: Okay, [our] number two engine blew. [There were] severe shudders and vibration through the airplane when it blew. Then we tried to pull the throttle back on number two, [but] it wouldn't come back. It was frozen. We shut it down [and] turned off the fuel in that [engine] [and we] pulled the fire handle on it, and we have only been able to hold direction control through power application . . . We're down to nine thousand [feet] now and we're tryin' to make Sioux City. We're gonna have to use alternate gear to get the [landing] gear down. I think we're gonna be kinda busy here. If there's anything I can talk to you about, I'll try to. If there's anything you can give for suggestions, give me a holler.

SIOUX CITY APPROACH: United two thirty-two heavy, there is a small airport at twelve o'clock and seven miles. The runway is four thousand feet long there.

CO-PILOT TO SIOUX CITY APPROACH: Hey, I'm controllin' it myself now. As soon as the captain gets back on, he'll give me a hand here. He's talking on the PA.

HAYNES TO CREW OFF THE PA: Okay, let's start this sucker down a little more.

JUMPSEAT FITCH: Okay, set your power a little bit.

CAPTAIN: Anybody have any ideas about

[what to do about the landing gear]? He's [the Engineer] is talking to SAM.

JUMPSEAT FITCH: Yeah, he's talking to SAM. I gonna alternate-gear you. Maybe that will even help you. [But] if there is no [hydraulic] fluid, I don't know how the outboard ailerons are going to help you.

HAYNES: How do you we get [landing] gear down?

JUMPSEAT FITCH: Well, they can freefall. The only thing is, we alternate the gear. We got the [landing gear] doors down?

HAYNES: Yep.

CO-PILOT: We're gonna have trouble stopping, too.

HAYNES: Oh, yeah. We don't have any brakes.

CO-PILOT: No brakes?

HAYNES: Well, we have some brakes [but not much].

JUMPSEAT FITCH: [Braking will be a] one-shot deal. Just mash it, mash it once. That's all you get. [To Haynes]: I'm gonna turn ya. [I'm gonna] give you a left turn back to the airport. Is that okay?

HAYNES: I got it. [To Sioux City]: Okay, United two thirty-two, we're startin to turn back to the airport. Since we have no hydraulics braking [it's] gonna really be a problem. [I] would suggest the [emergency] equipment be toward the far end of the runway. I think under the circumstances, regardless of the condition of the airplane when we stop, we're going to evacuate. So you might notify the ground crew [pretty much] that we're gonna do that.

SIOUX CITY APPROACH: United two thirty-two heavy, wilco, sir. If you can continue that left turn to about two-twenty heading, sir, that'll take you right to the airport.

CO-PILOT TO SIOUX CITY APPROACH: Two-twenty, roger.

HAYNES TO SIOUX CITY APPROACH: What's your ceiling right now?

JUMPSEAT FITCH: How far away are we from the airport? How far from the airport?

SIOUX CITY APPROACH: Ah, ceiling is four thousand, broken, and visibility's one five underneath it.

HAYNES: And the airport elevation?

SIOUX CITY APPROACH: One thousand ninety-eight [feet above sea level].

CO-PILOT: Well, [at] five thousand feet [of elevation] we ought to break out [of the clouds]. [To Haynes]: If you have any problem about the spoilers, Al, we won't have those either, will we?

HAYNES: I don't think that'll help. I'm off for just a second to buckle up.

CO-PILOT: All right.

JUMPSEAT FITCH: You can tell me what you need. Holler what you need . . .

HAYNES: What did SAM say? Good luck?

ENGINEER: He hasn't said anything.

HAYNES Okay, well forget them. Tell 'em you're leaving the air, and you're gonna come back up here and help us . . . and screw 'em. Ease her down just a little bit.

JUMPSEAT FITCH: When you get a chance ask them how far out we are?

HAYNES TO SIOUX CITY APPROACH: How far are we away from the airport now . . . ?

SIOUX CITY APPROACH: Thirty-five miles, and if you continue that left turn about another fifteen or twenty degrees it'll take you right to the runway.

HAYNES: Okay. We don't have a localizer or a glide slope, so . . .

SIOUX CITY APPROACH: Yes, sir. You're well too far north of it now.

HAYNES: Okay.

SAM: United two thirty-two, one more time. No hydraulic quantity, is that correct?

HAYNES Now we gotta level off a little bit. We're six thousand feet above the field right [now].

CREW: Yeah, right.

HAYNES About eighteen miles is where we want to be on the glide slope. We got about twelve miles to go before you want . . .

ENGINEER TO SAM: Affirmative, affirmative, affirmative.

JUMPSEAT FITCH: Oh, yeah, we'll be with power.

ENGINEER: Add a couple of knots [of speed] for those speeds up there.

JUMPSEAT FITCH: All right.

HAYNES: Anybody got any idea about puttin' the [landing] gear down right now?

JUMPSEAT FITCH: All right, I would. I would suggest . . .

HAYNES: Should we free fall it [the landing gear]?

CO-PILOT: Yeah, yeah. I got to get out of the way to get the door [to the manual release for the landing gear].

HAYNES: Put it down.

For the next few seconds the crew discusses the best way to get the landing gear down without hydraulic pressure. They will either use gravity and let the gear fall out of the wells, or they will crank it down.

HAYNES: Okay, put it down.

JUMPSEAT FITCH: I don't know. I don't have any great ideas.

CO-PILOT: Try it out.

SIOUX CITY APPROACH: United two thirty-two heavy, your present heading looks good.

HAYNES TO SIOUX CITY APPROACH: We'll see how close we can come to holding it.

CO-PILOT: Apply a little power.

JUMPSEAT FITCH: I can slow you down. Do you want to go to one eighty-five [knots].

HAYNES: Nope . . .

ENGINEER: [All] Green [on the landing gear down].

HAYNES: Go for it. Go ahead. Keep it at [one] eighty-five. Okay, start it down now. Ease back.

ENGINEER: Gear handle down. Gear handle down.

HAYNES: Okay, lock up and put everything away.

JUMPSEAT FITCH: Oh shit, there go the slats.

HAYNES: A little right turn. Don't have much to do. Sit down and lock up. Get up there and see what he is doin' for power.

CREW: Here we go.

CREW: I want to stay level if we can, if we're not too far out.

HAYNES: Okay, right turns. Level up first. Or level up our turn. Straighten out the turn. Get yourself all buttoned up.

COCKPIT: [Sound of a groan]

HAYNES: Level up here.

SIOUX CITY APPROACH: United two thirty-two heavy, can you still make the slight right turns?

HAYNES: Yeah. Right turns are no problem, just left turns . . .

SIOUX CITY APPROACH: Roger.

HAYNES: Well, momma. We'll [make or miss] those baseball games after all.

CO-PILOT: Are you in good and tight?

JUMPSEAT FITCH: I'm not in at all, Bill.

CO-PILOT: No, not you. But him . . .

JUMPSEAT FITCH: Yeah. It seems [we're] gonna have to keep more power on the right engine.

SIOUX CITY APPROACH: United two thirty-two heavy, sir, you are well too far north.

HAYNES: Pull it back. [To Sioux]: We know.

CREW: How many miles?

SIOUX CITY APPROACH: Two thirty-two heavy, your present heading is a little close, sir. Can you make a shallow left turn about ten degrees or so?

HAYNES I'll try.

CO-PILOT: Back on the controls.

JUMPSEAT FITCH: Got to get my glasses on or I can't see shit.

CO-PILOT TO SIOUX CITY APPROACH: Where's the airport?

SIOUX CITY APPROACH: United two thirty-two, the airport's currently twelve o'clock and two one [21] miles.

HAYNES: Twenty-one miles and thousand feet. We got to level off.

SIOUX CITY APPROACH: United two thirty-two heavy, you're gonna have to widen out just slightly to your left, sir, to make the turn to final and also it'll take you away from the city.

HAYNES: A little left bank. [To Sioux City]: Whatever you do, keep us away from the city. [To his crew]: Back, back.

JUMPSEAT FITCH: Hold this thing level if you can.

HAYNES: Level, baby, level, level . . .

ENGINEER: We're turning now.

JUMPSEAT FITCH: More power, more power, give 'em more power.

CO-PILOT: More power, full power.

JUMPSEAT FITCH: Power picks 'em up.

SIOUX CITY APPROACH: United two thirty-two heavy, fly heading one eight zero, one eighty . . .

HAYNES TO SIOUX CITY APPROACH: I don't think we can do that, but we'll try.

CREW: Right turn, throttle back.

HAYNES: Can we turn left?

SIOUX CITY APPROACH: You are currently one seven miles north-east of the airport. You're doing good . . .

HAYNES TO SIOUX CITY APPROACH: It has to be a right turn to one eighty. We can't do anything about it . . .

ENGINEER: Do you want this seat?

JUMPSEAT FITCH: Yes, do you mind?

ENGINEER: I don't mind. I think that you know what you're doing there before.

HAYNES: Level it off.

SIOUX CITY APPROACH: United two thirty-two heavy, there's a tower five miles off to your right side that's three thousand four hundred . . . in height.

CO-PILOT: Roger.

JUMPSEAT FITCH: Keep turning right, Al. Keep turning right.

HAYNES: You got to level this sucker off. The only thing that I was afraid of was putting the gear down in case we have to ditch.

SIOUX CITY APPROACH: United two thirty-two heavy, how steep a right turn can you make, sir?

HAYNES: About a thirty degree bank.

SIOUX CITY APPROACH: United two thirty-two heavy, roger. Turn right heading one eight zero.

CO-PILOT TO SIOUX CITY APPROACH: One eighty.

HAYNES: We got to level this sucker off. Come back, come back, come back.

JUMPSEAT FITCH: I got the tower [in view].

HAYNES: Come back, come back, all the way back.

JUMPSEAT FITCH: I can't handle that steep a bank. Can't handle that steep a bank.

SIOUX CITY APPROACH: United two thirty-two heavy, [I've] been advised [that] there is a four-lane highway up in that area, sir, if you can pick that up.

HAYNES TO SIOUX CITY APPROACH: Okay, we'll see what we can do here. We've already put down the gear and we're gonna have to be puttin' [down] on something solid if we can . . .

JUMPSEAT FITCH: Damn it. Wish we hadn't put that [landing] gear down.

ENGINEER: Ah, well.

JUMPSEAT FITCH: We don't know.

HAYNES: Just keep turnin' if you can.

JUMPSEAT FITCH: Which way do you want to go?

CREW: Right.

HAYNES: We got to go to one-eighty. Right is the only way to go. So we can't control the airplane. That way . . . [Sound of laughter]

CO-PILOT: All right, we're gonna have to try it straight ahead, Al. I think what we're gonna have to do . . .

SIOUX CITY APPROACH: United two thirty-two heavy, if you can hold that altitude, sir, the right turn to one-eighty would put you on about ten miles east of the airport.

HAYNES TO SIOUX CITY APPROACH: That's what we're tryin' to do.

CO-PILOT: Let's see if we can get a shallow descent, Al.

HAYNES: That's what I'm tryin' to do . . . Get this thing under control. When it starts up, push.

CO-PILOT: Okay. Here we go. Push hard, push hard.

JUMPSEAT FITCH: When the speed bleeds [creeps] back you'll catch it. Now, where do you want to go?

HAYNES: [I] Want to keep turnin' right. Want to go to the airport.

JUMPSEAT FITCH: You want to go to the airport.

HAYNES: I want to get as close to the airport as we can.

JUMPSEAT FITCH: Okay.

HAYNES: If we have to set this thing down in dirt, we set it in the dirt.

CREW: Speed's too low; watch the angle.

HAYNES TO CO-PILOT: Get on the air and tell them we got about four minutes to go.

CO-PILOT TO SIOUX CITY APPROACH: We've got about three or four minutes to go, [it] looks like.

HAYNES: PA system, PA system . . . Tell the passengers [to brace].

ENGINEER TO PASSENGERS ON PA SYSTEM: We have four minutes to touchdown, four minutes to touchdown . . .

SIOUX CITY APPROACH: United two thirty-two heavy, roger. Can you pick up a road or something up there?

CO-PILOT TO SIOUX CITY APPROACH: We're tryin' it. [We're] still [fluctuating our altitude] anywhere from two thousand [feet] up to fifteen hundred feet, down now, in waves.

JUMPSEAT FITCH TO HAYNES: Which way do you want to go?

HAYNES: Right, right, right. We gotta go . . .

CREW: Speed up!

JUMPSEAT FITCH: [The] airport's down there. Got it.

HAYNES: I don't see it yet.

CO-PILOT: Soon as it starts down, back we go . . .

CREW: Not too much back . . .

CO-PILOT: Okay, now you can bring 'em up.

CREW: Keep turning, keep turning, keep turning.

CO-PILOT: There's the airport.

SIOUX CITY APPROACH: United two thirty-two heavy, the airport is about eighteen miles south-east of your position, about two-twenty on the heading, but we're gonna need you southbound away from the city first. If you can hold one-eighty heading . . .

CO-PILOT TO SIOUX CITY APPROACH: We're tryin', tryin' to get to it right now.

JUMPSEAT FITCH: If I keep you about two hundred knots I seem to be able to get enough control . . .

SIOUX CITY APPROACH: United two thirty-two heavy, advise if you can pick up a road or anything where you can possibly land it on that.

HAYNES TO SIOUX CITY APPROACH: Okay,

we're a hundred eighty degree heading. Now what do you want?

SIOUX CITY APPROACH: United two thirty-two, if you can hold the altitude, the one-eighty heading will work fine for about seven miles.

HAYNES TO SIOUX CITY APPROACH: Okay, we're tryin' to turn back. [To Jumpseat]: Forward, make a left turn, left . . .

JUMPSEAT FITCH: No left at all.

HAYNES: No left at all?

JUMPSEAT FITCH: I'll give you some.

CO-PILOT: Okay, now it's . . .

HAYNES: Back, back back back . . . Forward forward forward . . . Won't this be a fun landing? Back . . . [sound of laughter].

SIOUX CITY APPROACH: United two thirty-two heavy, can you hold that heading, sir?

CO-PILOT TO SIOUX CITY APPROACH: Yeah, we're on it now for a little while.

SIOUX CITY APPROACH: United two thirty-two heavy, roger. That heading will put you currently fifteen miles north-east of the airport. If you can hold that, it'll put you on about a three-mile final.

CO-PILOT: Okay, we're givin' it heck.

HAYNES: I'll tell you what. I'll write off your damn PC [Pilot Certificate] if we make this

. . . *when* we make this. Hold the heading if you can . . . That's fine. Turn left. Help me turn left so we know what it's doing. Back back back . . .

SIOUX CITY APPROACH: United two thirty-two heavy, the airport's currently twelve o'clock and one three [13] miles.

CO-PILOT TO SIOUX CITY APPROACH: Okay, we're lookin' for it.

HAYNES: Forward forward forward . . .

CO-PILOT: Twelve o'clock at thirteen miles. We have to start down, but . . .

JUMPSEAT FITCH: Ask what the field elevation is.

HAYNES TO SIOUX CITY APPROACH: Field elevation is what again?

CO-PILOT: A thousand eighty.

SIOUX CITY APPROACH: Ah, eleven hundred feet, one thousand one hundred . . .

HAYNES: Okay, thank you.

JUMPSEAT FITCH: Let's start down. We have to ease it down.

HAYNES TO SIOUX CITY APPROACH: We're startin' down a little bit now. We got a little better control of the elevator.

SIOUX CITY APPROACH: United two thirty-two heavy, roger. The airport's currently at your one o'clock position, one zero [10] miles.

HAYNES: Ease it down, ease it down . . .

COCKPIT: [Sound of groan, sound of exhalation]

JUMPSEAT FITCH: I got the runway, if you don't . . .

HAYNES: I don't . . . Come back, come back.

JUMPSEAT FITCH: It's off to the right over there.

CO-PILOT: Right there. Let's see if we can hold [a descent rate of] five hundred feet a minute.

SIOUX CITY APPROACH: United two thirty-two heavy, if you can't make the airport, sir, there is an interstate that runs north to south, to the east side of the airport. It's a four-lane interstate.

JUMPSEAT FITCH: See? We got [the] tower [in sight] right here at our one o'clock low . . .

HAYNES TO SIOUX CITY APPROACH: We're just passing it [the highway] right now. We're gonna try for the air[port]. [To jumpseat] Is that the runway right there?

CREW: Right.

HAYNES TO SIOUX CITY APPROACH: We have the runway in sight. We have the runway in sight. We have the runway in sight. We'll be with you shortly. Thanks a lot for your help.

JUMPSEAT FITCH: Bring it on down . . . Ease 'er down.

CO-PILOT: Oh, baby.

JUMPSEAT FITCH: Ease her down.

HAYNES: Tell 'em [the passengers] that we're just two minutes from landing.

SIOUX CITY APPROACH: United two thirty-two heavy, the wind's currently three six zero at one one three sixty at eleven. You're cleared to land on any runway . . .

HAYNES TO SIOUX CITY APPROACH: [Laughter] Roger. [Laughter] You want to be particular and make it a runway, huh?

ENGINEER TO PASSENGERS ON PA SYSTEM: Two minutes.

In the passenger cabin, the Attendants begin shouting for passengers to get their heads down. The first Flight Attendant yells commands.

JUMPSEAT FITCH: What's the wind?

HAYNES TO SIOUX CITY APPROACH: Say the wind one more time.

SIOUX CITY APPROACH: Wind's zero one zero at one one . . .

CO-PILOT: Yeah, we want to go down.

JUMPSEAT FITCH: Yeah, I can see the runway, but I got to keep control on ya.

CO-PILOT: Pull it off a little.

HAYNES: See if you can get us a left turn.

CO-PILOT: Left turn just a hair, Al.

HAYNES TO SIOUX CITY APPROACH: Okay, we're all three talking at once. Say it [the wind] again one more time.

SIOUX CITY APPROACH: Zero one zero at one one, and there is a runway that's closed, sir, that could probably work to he south. It runs north-east to south-west.

HAYNES TO SIOUX CITY APPROACH: We're pretty well lined up on this one here . . .

JUMPSEAT FITCH: I'll pull the spoilers [speedbrakes] on the touch[down].

HAYNES: Get the brakes on with me.

SIOUX CITY APPROACH: United two thirty-two heavy, roger, sir. That's a closed runway, sir, that'll work, sir. We're gettin' the equipment off the runway. They'll line up for that one.

HAYNES TO SIOUX CITY APPROACH: How long is it?

SIOUX CITY APPROACH: Sixty-six hundred feet [6,600 feet], six thousand six hundred. Equipment's comin' off.

HAYNES TO CREW: Pull the power back. That's right. Pull the left one [throttle] back.

CO-PILOT: Pull the left one back.

SIOUX CITY APPROACH: At the end of the runway it's just wide open field.

CREW: Left throttle, left, left, left, left . . .

CREW: God!

COCKPIT: [Sound of impact]

END OF TAPE

In the passenger cabin, the first Flight Attendant described the impact as 'a wind coming over a field and blowing down the grass'. All the passengers' heads were down. A couple of passengers had put up their heads prior to impact, and the Flight Attendants yelled at them to keep their heads down. There was an 'unbelievable noise' during the impact, the first Flight Attendant recalled. She saw two overhead bins begin to open, and she felt a fireball pass through the cabin. The fireball came up the left side of the cabin and went three quarters of the way over the first Flight Attendant, and a few seconds later the airplane came to a stop. She was upside down and pressing against her seatbelt. She released her seatbelt with difficulty. She slid down and stood up on the debris of the airplane, but she was able to stand upright.

She saw a man lying forward of where she was standing, and his ankles were wedged in a crevice of the wreckage. She pulled him free. She saw a crack of light and heard passengers say there was an opening. She went to the opening and started to push passengers out. She thought the entire area of the airplane forward of her jumpseat in the first-class cabin was gone. She said that there were 'no doors, there was nothing recognizable'. She saw a grey-black smoke coming from the mid cabin. It was 'swirling, rolling forward'. She exited the airplane into a cornfield and ran from the airplane. She tried to find a clear area where she could gather together the survivors, but because of the height of the cornstalks, she could not see a clear area. She 'started tramping down the corn stalks'. She saw another Flight Attendant and he seemed dazed.

Flight Attendant number two remembered the airplane hitting the ground this way: 'kind of screeching back and forth and back and forth and the lights going out and coming back on'. There was a lot of 'skidding around'. She did not remember anything after that. She had not buckled in at impact. She was found with dirt in her mouth and nose in an area where other people were not alive. She was seriously injured.

Flight 232 had touched down on the threshold and to the left of the centerline on closed Runway 22. The first contact with the ground was made by the right wingtip. The right main landing gear broke the concrete beyond the first impact point. The airplane skidded off Runway 22, then flipped over. The main fuselage section stopped upside down in a corn field between Runway 17 and Taxiway L. Both wings were still attached, though most of the right wing had broken off. The tail section had broken off at the first impact and continued to slide and tumble down the runway and came to a stop on Taxiway L.

The main fuselage section and the tail section came to a stop 3,650 feet from the point of first impact.

One passenger, a 36-year-old man, had assumed the brace position prior to impact, which he described as a little harder than a normal landing. But the second impact was 'so hard that I thought I would go through the seat cushion'. There was a 'tremendous' explosion, he said later. And he was thrown around in his seat. The lights went out. The floor emergency lights flickered, then went off. He saw smoke and there was a 'terrible smell'. He was struck by other passengers who had fallen from their seats. Suitcases tumbled from the overhead bins. He got out of his seat and walked on the ceiling through an opening in the fuselage.

Just before impact, a 25-year-old mother placed her 23-month-old son on the floor and covered him with a blanket. She wedged a pillow between his head and the cabin wall, then took the brace position and held her son down with one hand on his legs and her other hand on his chest. The plane hit the ground and it rolled to the right, she remembered. She heard metal scraping, and dirt and plastic flew around her. 'My son flew up in the air, and I managed to grab ahold of him around the waist,' she said. 'He struck his head several times before the plane came to a stop, and several times I had to pull him back into my arms as he slid out of my grip.' When the plane stopped, they were upside down, and she was holding onto her son. When she released her seatbelt, they fell to the ceiling of the upside down cabin. She landed on her shoulder, and her son hit his head. A man seated next to her helped her up and pushed her toward the hole in the fuselage that other passengers were using to evacuate the wreckage. She walked barefoot through plastic and luggage. 'As I exited,' she said, 'I looked to my right and saw an elderly grey hair [sic] woman still buckled in her seat. I pointed her out to the person behind me, but I saw no movement from the lady.'

There were 296 passengers and crew aboard Flight 232. 185 people survived the accident, including seven Flight Attendants and the three cockpit members. Fatalities included 110 passengers and one Flight Attendant.

GLOSSARY

ACARS: Air-to-Ground Communication and Reporting System. Cockpit messaging system from ground to aircraft that can be read as a display or can be printed out in a cockpit printer. Among other messages received on ACARS are the connecting gate numbers that the cabin crew will often read out to passengers before landing.

ANNUNCIATOR LIGHT: A caution or warning light on the panel of the cockpit called the annunciator panel. There is an annunciator light for every system on the aircraft.

APU: Auxiliary Power Unit. An engine aboard the aircraft, usually located in the tail, for the generation of electrical and hydraulic power when the main engines are shut off.

ARMED: To set; spoilers armed, for instance, indicates that the spoilers have been programed to deploy automatically without pilot involvement after landing when the main wheels are spinning at a certain rate of speed.

AUTOPILOT: Autopilot takes directions from the flight director, which commands the aircraft from take-off to landing. The autopilot takes raw data and gives the aircraft a perfect flight path.

BEFORE LANDING CHECKLIST: Landing gear is down and there is a three-light verification that gear is down. The spoiler handle is armed, and when the aircraft touches down, the spoilers deploy – i.e. they elevate on the wing to kill lift – when the main wheels reach a certain set speed. When the spoiler is deployed while the aircraft is still in flight, it is referred to as a speedbrake and functions the same by spoiling lift and slowing down the aircraft.

BLEEDS: Use of heated air in a jet engine to pressurize and heat the cabin and operate pneumatic systems; when bleeds in the engine are open, air is supplied to these systems.

BUG: A setting on the rim of several instruments in the cockpit to remind the pilot of reference speeds and altitudes. Bug speed, for instance, is the aircraft's determined approach speed based on the weight of the airplane. There are other bug speeds, but approach speed is the most important one.

CHARLIE CHARLIE: Yes, yes.

COPY: 'I understand.' Usually a remark made by the cockpit crew while communicating with flight controllers on the ground.

CROSS FEEDS: Valves that permit the transfer of fuel from one tank to another.

DME: Distance Measuring Equipment. Provides a display in nautical miles of distance from the VOR, or an ILS (Instrument Landing System) beam at an airport.

FLAPS: Trailing edge devices on the wings that increase the lift of the wings on take-off and especially on landing.

FLIGHT DIRECTOR: A computer system that flies the airplane automatically and corrects for wind and drift and flies a course or beam, laterally and vertically. It is programed at the start of flights to operate the airplane through to the end of the flight and with this responsibility it directs the airplane's autopilot.

FORTY-FORTY LAND: Flap selector is mechanically selected to full or 40° and the electronic indicator says it is 40°. Both indicators are read out and spoken by the cockpit crew before landing.

GLIDESLOPE CAPTURE: On an Instrument Landing System (ILS) approach to a runway, when the pilot has captured the glideslope, the aircraft is at the proper altitude and on a correct heading for a safe landing. Aircraft is on the glide path, which means the aircraft is at a distance to pick up the Instrument Landing System's altitude to come down on the runway safely.

HEAVY: An air traffic controller's term for a larger aircraft, usually a wide-bodied Boeing 747, DC-10, L-1011, with a gross take-off weight in excess of 255,000 pounds.

HYDRAULICS: The mechanism (hydraulic fluid under pressure) that controls surfaces (elevators, rudders, ailerons, flaps, etc.) on the aircraft; as in 'Do we have hydraulics?'

IDENT: Identify the aircraft to Air Traffic Controllers by pushing a button inside the cockpit that illuminates a transponder dot on radar screens beside which are an identification number and altitude. Same as 'squawk'.

LNAV: Lateral Navigation. Modern airplanes, like a Boeing 767, have LNAV and VNAV functions. LNAV navigates an aircraft automatically in a lateral direction. VNAV will navigate the aircraft automatically in a vertical direction. Both LNAV and VNAV are computer generated.

LOCALIZER: Part of the Instrument Landing System (ILS), an electronic beam that indicates the runway center line.

MINIMUMS: Levels of altitude and visibility below which the aircraft cannot safely fly.

OUTER MARKER: Part of the ILS. A point of instrument light in the cockpit and a sound warning to indicate the final approach that tells pilots that they have begun the serious part of the approach, or glide slope capture or outer marker. Next is the middle marker reached at about two hundred feet above the ground. An inner marker exists for some approaches.

POSITIVE [CLIMB RATE]: On take-off, before the landing gear is raised, there must be an indication of a positive climb rate by a vertical velocity indicator that shows a climb, and an altimeter that shows a climb in feet.

PUMPS ARE UP: Hydraulic pumps are on high before takeoff and landing. Jets take off and land with pumps at a high system pressure to raise the heavy landing gear, and above 18,000 feet the pumps are set at a lower position for cruise.

ROTATE: Speed required for the pilot to lift the aircraft's nose off the runway during take-off, depending on the aircraft's weight. It is used as a command to 'rotate', or lift the nose when the required speed has been reached.

RUDDER RATIO: Limits the amount of rudder force that can be used at high speed. The ratio is smaller at high altitudes and greater at lower altitudes, especially when the aircraft is landing.

SIGMET: Significant Meteorological Advisory; usually indicating severe weather.

SINK RATE: A rate of descent.

SLATS: Leading edge devices on the wings which give the wings additional lift and act in concert usually with the trailing edge wing flaps.

SPOILERS: Surfaces on the tops of the wings that are extended after touchdown to kill lift on the wing; these spoilers are deployed sometimes in-flight to 'brake' the airplane and reduce altitude, and in this use they are referred to as Speed Brakes.

SPOOL UP: Increase the rpms (revolutions per minute) of the engines.

STALL: Airspeed at which the aircraft's wings can no longer maintain lift to prevent the aircraft from falling. To recover from a stall, the aircraft must have sufficient altitude to regain adequate airspeed by putting the nose down and adding power.

STICK SHAKER: A warning device on commercial aircraft that literally shakes the control column in the pilot's hands to warn of the approach of the aircraft's stall speed.

TCAS: Traffic Collision Avoidance System, which identifies other nearby aircrafts' altitude and direction. If there is a conflict, a voice warning commands, 'Traffic, traffic'.

THREE GREEN: All three sets of landing gear are down and locked.

TRANSPONDER: An electronic device aboard aircraft that communicates a signal to Air Traffic Control's radar and other aircraft indicating an identifying number and usually the aircraft's altitude and sometimes its direction.

VECTORS: Compass headings issued by ground controllers.

VISUAL ADVISORY WARNING: Another term of a annunciator light that goes on to warn of a system failure or malfunction.

VEE ONE: A decision speed on take-off at which the pilot can either stop the aircraft on the runway if there is an engine failure or the pilot can take off and clear the end of the runway by 35 feet.

VEE ROTATE: When the aircraft has reached sufficient speed to pull the nose off the runway.

VEE TWO: A speed at which the aircraft can continue to climb on one engine in the case of an engine failure during this critical part of flight.

VOR: Very high frequency omnidirectional radio range. An old navigational aid described as the radial spokes in a 360°wheel.

WAKE VORTEX: Vortices created by the lift of a wing. A dangerous time is when a plane is 'slow and clean', when the flaps are still up and it is ready for landing; wings are working their hardest. This creates a violent, spiralling wind called a vortex, like a little tornado. It is vicious, and a larger airplane can upset a smaller airplane with a wake vortex.

YAW DAMPER: A mechanical device on the control surfaces in the tail of the aircraft that helps alleviate an aircraft's tendency to yaw left or right which can induce a 'Dutch Roll'.

ACKNOWLEDGEMENTS

I would like to thank Ted Lapactkiewicz, the Deputy Director of Public Affairs at the National Transportation Safety Board (NTSB) in Washington, D.C. for his help and kindness in gathering together these materials. Also Bryan Reich, a First Officer with American Airlines, for vetting the manuscript with a professional eye.

INDEX